Family Favorites

*Tried-and-True Recipes
to Bring Everyone
Together*

ZELDA BARBER

The presentation of the information is without contract or any type of guarantee assurance. The trademarks that are used are without any consent, and the publication of the trademark is without permission or backing by the trademark owner. All trademarks and brands within this book are for clarifying purposes only and are the owned by the owners themselves, not affiliated with this document.

Table of Contents

Chapter 1

Introduction

The Magic of Family Meals

Family meals have long been considered a cornerstone of family life, a sacred time when members gather to share not just food, but stories, laughter, and a sense of belonging. The magic of family meals lies in their ability to strengthen familial bonds, foster communication, and build lasting memories. In modern times, with the hustle and bustle of daily life, prioritizing these mealtime gatherings can be challenging, but the benefits they offer make the effort worthwhile.

One of the most significant advantages of family meals is the opportunity they provide for meaningful communication. In a world dominated by digital interactions, face-to-face conversations are increasingly rare. Family meals create a natural setting for open dialogue, where everyone can share their experiences, thoughts, and feelings. This practice helps to foster a sense of security and trust among family members, as they know they have a dedicated time to connect with each other.

Children, in particular, benefit immensely from regular family meals. Studies have shown that kids who participate in family dinners are more likely to perform better academically, have higher self-esteem, and exhibit lower rates of depression and anxiety. The structured environment of a family meal provides children with a reliable routine, which is crucial for their emotional and psychological development. Additionally, these meals offer an opportunity for parents to model positive behaviors and social skills, such as manners, active listening, and respectful conversation.

The nutritional benefits of family meals should not be overlooked. Families that eat together tend to consume healthier, more balanced diets. Home-cooked meals are generally more nutritious than fast food or pre-packaged options, as they often include fresh ingredients and fewer processed components. When families dine together, they are more likely to prepare meals that include a variety of food groups, promoting better overall health. Furthermore, children who regularly eat with their families are less likely to develop unhealthy eating habits, such as excessive snacking or skipping meals.

Family meals also serve as an excellent platform for teaching life skills. Cooking together can be a fun and educational experience for children, who learn valuable skills such as meal planning, food preparation, and kitchen safety. These skills are not only practical but also encourage a sense of responsibility and independence. As children grow older, their involvement in meal preparation can increase, fostering a deeper appreciation for the effort that goes into creating a meal and the importance of contributing to family life.

The social aspect of family meals is another key component of their magic. Sharing a meal encourages a sense of community and togetherness. It is a time for family members to celebrate achievements, support each other through challenges, and create shared memories. The ritual of eating together can become a cherished tradition, offering a sense of continuity and stability in an ever-changing world. For families with diverse schedules, setting aside specific times for meals can help ensure that everyone feels connected and valued.

Incorporating family meals into a busy lifestyle requires intentionality and planning. One effective strategy is to establish a regular mealtime that works for everyone's schedule. This might mean having breakfast together a few times a week if dinner isn't feasible. Flexibility is key; the goal is to find a routine that allows for consistent family interaction. It's also important to create a pleasant dining environment, free from distractions such as television or smartphones. This helps to keep the focus on the conversation and the shared experience.

Another way to enhance the experience of family meals is by involving everyone in the process. From meal planning to cooking and setting the table, each family member can play a role. This not only lightens the workload but also fosters a sense of teamwork and collaboration. Encouraging children to participate in decision-making, such as choosing recipes or ingredients, can make them more enthusiastic about the meals and more likely to try new foods.

The benefits of family meals extend beyond the immediate family unit. Inviting extended family members or friends to join in can enrich the experience, introducing new perspectives and traditions. This practice helps to strengthen social networks and create a broader sense of community. Additionally, it provides an opportunity for children to learn about different cultures and customs, promoting a sense of diversity and inclusion.

While the idea of family meals conjures images of perfectly orchestrated dinners, it's important to remember that the goal is connection, not perfection. Meals don't have to be elaborate or time-consuming to be meaningful. Simple, quick-to-prepare dishes can be just as effective in bringing the family together. The focus should be on the quality of the interactions rather than the complexity of the meal.

In situations where gathering for a meal every day isn't possible, families can still benefit from occasional special meals. Weekend brunches, Sunday dinners, or holiday feasts can become treasured traditions. These events provide an opportunity to slow down, savor the moment, and reconnect with each other. They can also serve as a reminder of the importance of family time, encouraging everyone to prioritize these moments despite busy schedules.

In conclusion, the magic of family meals lies in their power to bring people together, foster communication, and create lasting memories. They offer a multitude of benefits, from improved nutrition and life skills to enhanced emotional well-being and social connections. By prioritizing family meals and approaching them with flexibility and intentionality, families can strengthen their bonds and build a foundation of love and support that will endure through the years. The effort invested in sharing

regular meals is a small price to pay for the profound
and lasting impact they have on family life. Family
meals also provide an invaluable opportunity for
cultural transmission. Through the foods prepared
and shared, families can pass down culinary
traditions, recipes, and cultural practices that define
their heritage. Each dish can tell a story, linking the
present to the past and preserving the unique identity
of the family. This transmission of knowledge fosters a
sense of pride and belonging among family members,
giving them a deeper understanding of their roots and
a stronger connection to their ancestry.

How to Use This Book

Learning a new skill or improving an existing one can
be a transformative journey. This book is designed to
be your companion on that journey, providing you
with the tools and knowledge you need to succeed.
Whether you're a complete beginner or looking to
refine your skills, this guide will help you navigate the
complexities and nuances of the subject. To get the
most out of this book, it's essential to understand how
to use it effectively.

The structure of this book is carefully crafted to build
your knowledge in a logical and progressive manner.
Each chapter is dedicated to a specific aspect of the
subject, starting with the basics and gradually moving
towards more advanced concepts. This approach
ensures that you have a solid foundation before
tackling more complex topics. Therefore, it's
recommended to read the chapters in order, especially
if you're new to the subject. Skipping ahead might

leave you confused or missing critical information that's necessary for understanding later sections.

One of the key features of this book is its practical approach. Each chapter includes real-world examples, case studies, and exercises that are designed to reinforce the concepts discussed. These practical elements are crucial for turning theoretical knowledge into actionable skills. Make sure to engage actively with these sections. When you encounter an exercise, take the time to complete it thoroughly. These exercises are not just supplementary; they are integral to your learning process. By applying what you've learned in a practical context, you'll deepen your understanding and retain the information more effectively.

To illustrate the importance of practical application, consider the story of Maria. Maria was new to the field and felt overwhelmed by the sheer amount of information she needed to learn. She decided to follow the book's structure and diligently worked through each exercise. By the time she reached the more advanced chapters, she realized that her practical experience from the exercises had given her the confidence and competence to tackle complex problems with ease. Maria's story underscores the value of taking the exercises seriously and using them as opportunities to practice and refine your skills.

Another crucial aspect of using this book is reflection. After completing each chapter, take a moment to reflect on what you've learned. Ask yourself questions like: What new concepts did I discover? How can these concepts be applied in real-world scenarios?

What challenges did I encounter, and how did I overcome them? Reflection helps to consolidate your learning and provides insights into your progress. It also allows you to identify areas where you might need further practice or clarification.

It's also beneficial to keep a learning journal as you work through the book. In your journal, jot down key takeaways, personal insights, and any questions that arise. This practice not only aids in retention but also serves as a valuable resource that you can refer back to. Over time, your journal will become a personalized guide that captures your growth and development in the subject.

The book is also designed to be a flexible resource that you can return to whenever needed. If you encounter a particular challenge or need a refresher on a specific topic, don't hesitate to revisit earlier chapters. The comprehensive index and clear chapter headings make it easy to find the information you need quickly. This feature is particularly useful as you progress and start applying your knowledge in real-world situations. Having the ability to quickly reference key concepts will enhance your problem-solving capabilities and boost your confidence.

Engaging with the community can significantly enhance your learning experience. Many concepts and skills covered in this book can benefit from discussion and collaboration with others who share similar interests. Look for online forums, local meetups, or study groups where you can exchange ideas, ask questions, and receive feedback. Sharing your experiences and learning from others can provide new perspectives and deepen your understanding. It's also an excellent way to stay motivated and inspired throughout your learning journey.

Balancing theory and practice is essential for mastering the subject. While it's tempting to focus solely on practical exercises, having a strong theoretical foundation is equally important. The theory provides context and understanding, which are necessary for making informed decisions and solving problems effectively. As you progress through the book, make sure to pay equal attention to both the theoretical explanations and the practical applications. This balanced approach will equip you with a well-rounded skill set that's both deep and broad.

For example, consider the case of John, who initially skipped the theoretical sections to jump straight into the exercises. While he became proficient at executing specific tasks, he often found himself struggling to understand why certain techniques worked better than others. By revisiting the theoretical chapters, John was able to grasp the underlying principles, which in turn improved his practical skills and decision-making abilities. John's experience highlights the importance of integrating both theory and practice in your learning process.

Time management is another critical factor in using this book effectively. Set aside dedicated time for study and practice, and create a consistent schedule that you can stick to. Consistency is key to making steady progress. Even short, regular study sessions can be more effective than infrequent, lengthy sessions. Find a routine that works for you and make it a habit. Remember, learning is a marathon, not a sprint. Pace yourself, and don't rush through the material. Give yourself ample time to absorb and understand each concept before moving on to the next.

Additionally, don't be afraid to seek help if you encounter difficulties. Whether it's reaching out to a mentor, joining a study group, or participating in online forums, there are numerous resources available to support you. Asking for help is a sign of commitment to your learning journey, not a weakness. By leveraging the knowledge and experience of others, you can overcome obstacles more efficiently and gain valuable insights that might not be apparent from the book alone.

Finally, celebrate your progress and achievements along the way. Learning a new skill can be challenging, and it's important to acknowledge your efforts and milestones. Whether it's completing a particularly difficult exercise, understanding a complex concept, or successfully applying your knowledge in a real-world scenario, take the time to recognize and celebrate your accomplishments. This positive reinforcement will keep you motivated and reinforce the value of your hard work.

In conclusion, using this book effectively requires a combination of structured reading, active engagement with practical exercises, reflection, and consistent practice. By following these strategies, you'll be well-equipped to master the subject and achieve your learning goals. Remember, the journey of learning is as important as the destination. Embrace the process, stay curious, and enjoy the experience of acquiring new knowledge and skills. As you embark on this learning journey, it's also important to cultivate a mindset of resilience and perseverance. There will be moments of frustration and difficulty, but these are natural parts of the learning process. Embrace challenges as opportunities to grow and learn. When you encounter obstacles, remind yourself of your progress and the reasons why you started this journey in the first place. Keeping your long-term goals in mind can provide the motivation you need to push through tough times.

Essential Kitchen Tools

A well-equipped kitchen is the cornerstone of any culinary endeavor. Whether you are a novice cook venturing into the world of home cooking or a seasoned chef looking to refine your toolkit, having the right kitchen tools can make all the difference. The right tools not only streamline the cooking process but also enhance the quality and consistency of your dishes. This chapter delves into the essential kitchen tools that every cook should have and how to use them effectively.

First and foremost, a good set of knives is indispensable in any kitchen. At a minimum, you should have a chef's knife, a paring knife, and a serrated bread knife. The chef's knife is your workhorse, suitable for most chopping, slicing, and dicing tasks. Investing in a high-quality chef's knife can significantly improve your efficiency and precision. The paring knife is perfect for smaller tasks such as peeling fruits and vegetables or trimming fat from meat. Meanwhile, the serrated bread knife is essential for slicing through crusty bread and delicate pastries without crushing them. Regularly honing your knives and occasionally having them professionally sharpened will keep them in top condition.

A sturdy cutting board is another kitchen essential. Opt for a large cutting board made of wood or plastic. Wood is gentle on your knives and has natural antibacterial properties, while plastic boards are easier to sanitize. Having multiple cutting boards can prevent cross-contamination, especially when handling raw meat and vegetables simultaneously. Remember to clean and sanitize your cutting boards thoroughly after each use to maintain a hygienic cooking environment.

Measuring cups and spoons are critical for ensuring accuracy in your recipes, particularly when baking. Dry measuring cups are designed for ingredients like flour and sugar, while liquid measuring cups are essential for wet ingredients such as milk and oil. Measuring spoons come in various sizes and are invaluable for small quantities of spices and extracts. Accuracy in measurement can be the difference between a successful dish and a culinary disaster, especially in baking where precise ratios are crucial.

Mixing bowls in various sizes are fundamental for combining ingredients. Stainless steel bowls are durable and versatile, suitable for everything from mixing batters to marinating meats. Glass bowls are also a great option as they are microwave-safe and allow you to see the contents clearly. Having a range of sizes ensures you have the right bowl for any task, whether you're whisking eggs or tossing a salad.

A set of pots and pans is essential for cooking a variety of dishes. At the very least, you should have a large stockpot for soups and stews, a medium-sized saucepan for sauces and grains, and a skillet for frying and sautéing. Non-stick pans are great for delicate items like eggs and pancakes, while stainless steel or cast iron skillets provide excellent heat distribution for searing and browning. Investing in high-quality cookware can improve your cooking results and ensure your tools last for years.

Baking sheets and pans are necessary if you plan to do any baking or roasting. A standard baking sheet, often called a half-sheet pan, is perfect for cookies, roasted vegetables, and sheet pan dinners. Additionally, having a muffin tin, loaf pan, and cake pans in various sizes will cover most of your baking needs. Silicone baking mats can be a worthwhile investment, as they provide a non-stick surface and make cleanup easier.

A reliable set of kitchen utensils is essential for various cooking tasks. This includes a spatula, wooden spoon, tongs, and a whisk. A heat-resistant spatula is ideal for scraping and mixing, while a wooden spoon is perfect for stirring hot dishes without damaging your cookware. Tongs are versatile tools for flipping meats, tossing salads, and serving food. A whisk is indispensable for blending ingredients smoothly, whether you're making sauces or whipping cream.

A food thermometer is an often-overlooked tool that can significantly improve your cooking. Ensuring that meat, poultry, and seafood are cooked to the appropriate temperature is crucial for both safety and flavor. An instant-read digital thermometer provides quick and accurate readings, helping you avoid undercooked or overcooked dishes. Knowing the correct temperatures for different types of meat can elevate your cooking from good to exceptional.

A colander or strainer is essential for draining pasta, rinsing vegetables, and straining broths. Stainless steel colanders are durable and easy to clean, while mesh strainers are perfect for finer tasks like rinsing quinoa or sifting flour. Having both a large colander and a fine-mesh strainer will cover most of your needs.

A blender or food processor can be a game-changer in the kitchen. Blenders are excellent for smoothies, soups, and sauces, while food processors are invaluable for tasks like chopping vegetables, making dough, and grinding nuts. A high-quality blender or food processor can save time and effort, allowing you to create complex recipes with minimal hassle.

A kitchen scale is an invaluable tool for precise measurement, particularly in baking. While measuring cups and spoons are useful, a scale provides the most accurate measurements, ensuring consistency in your recipes. Many professional chefs and bakers rely on scales to achieve perfect results every time. Investing in a digital kitchen scale can elevate your baking and cooking, ensuring each dish is made to perfection.

Having a set of mixing spoons, preferably wooden or silicone, is essential for stirring and combining ingredients without scratching your cookware. Wooden spoons are particularly useful for their durability and resistance to heat. Silicone spoons offer the added benefit of being non-stick and heat-resistant, making them ideal for a variety of cooking tasks.

A rolling pin is indispensable for anyone who enjoys baking. Whether you're rolling out cookie dough, pie crusts, or pizza dough, a good rolling pin can make the task much easier. Wooden rolling pins are traditional and reliable, while newer models with non-stick surfaces can simplify the process even further. Ensure your rolling pin is comfortable to use and easy to clean.

Storage containers are crucial for keeping your kitchen organized and your food fresh. Glass or BPA-free plastic containers with airtight lids are ideal for storing leftovers, meal prep, and pantry staples. Having a variety of sizes will ensure you have the right container for every need. Clear containers allow you to see the contents easily, helping you keep track of what you have on hand.

An immersion blender is a versatile tool that can be used directly in pots and bowls, making it perfect for pureeing soups, sauces, and smoothies. Unlike traditional blenders, immersion blenders are easy to clean and store. They are particularly useful for tasks that require a quick blend without the hassle of transferring ingredients to a separate appliance.

Egg beaters and hand mixers are invaluable for tasks that require vigorous mixing, such as whipping cream or beating egg whites. While a whisk can handle many tasks, an electric hand mixer provides speed and consistency, ensuring your batters and doughs are perfectly mixed without the effort.

A mandolin slicer can save time and ensure uniform slices, whether you're making potato chips, julienning vegetables, or slicing fruits. While it requires careful handling due to its sharp blades, a mandoline can produce precise cuts that are difficult to achieve with a knife. Adjustable settings allow you to choose the thickness of your slices, making it a versatile addition to your kitchen.

Lastly, don't overlook the importance of a well-organized kitchen. Keeping your tools and utensils in designated places ensures you can find what you need quickly and easily. Drawer dividers, utensil holders, and wall-mounted racks can help you maintain order and efficiency in your cooking space. An organized kitchen not only makes cooking more enjoyable but also helps maintain a clean and safe environment.

In conclusion, equipping your kitchen with the right tools is an investment in your culinary success. Each tool has a specific purpose and, when used correctly, can enhance your cooking experience and the quality of your dishes. By understanding the essential kitchen tools and how to use them effectively, you can tackle any recipe with confidence and creativity. Remember, the right tools can transform your kitchen from a place of routine meal preparation into a haven of culinary exploration and innovation. As you build your collection of kitchen tools, it's important to periodically reassess and maintain them to ensure they remain in optimal condition. Proper care and maintenance of your tools will extend their lifespan and keep them performing at their best.

Stocking Your Pantry

A well-stocked pantry is the foundation of efficient and enjoyable home cooking. It provides the flexibility to whip up a meal without constant trips to the grocery store and ensures you have essential ingredients on hand for a wide variety of dishes. Understanding how to stock your pantry involves more than just buying a random assortment of goods; it requires thoughtful planning, knowledge of essential items, and an eye for organization.

Begin with the basics—those staple ingredients that form the backbone of countless recipes. Flour, sugar, salt, and pepper are non-negotiable essentials. Flour, whether all-purpose or a mix of types such as whole wheat and bread flour, is the cornerstone of baking, thickening sauces, and breading proteins. Sugar, both granulated and brown, is crucial for baking and balancing flavors in savory dishes. Salt enhances the natural flavors of food, and kosher or sea salt is often preferred for its texture and taste. Freshly ground black pepper adds a depth of flavor that pre-ground varieties simply can't match.

Next, consider the variety of oils and vinegars you'll need. A good extra-virgin olive oil is indispensable for dressings, marinades, and low-heat cooking.

Vegetable oil or canola oil, with their higher smoke points, are better suited for frying and high-heat applications. Coconut oil can be a versatile addition, useful in both savory dishes and baking. Vinegars, including apple cider, balsamic, and white wine vinegar, bring acidity and brightness to dressings, sauces, and marinades. Each type of vinegar has unique properties that can elevate a dish, from the sweetness of balsamic to the tanginess of apple cider vinegar.

Grains and legumes are also vital components of a well-stocked pantry. Rice, both long-grain varieties like basmati and short-grain types like arborio, is a versatile base for many meals. Quinoa, barley, and couscous can add variety and nutritional value to your diet. Dried pasta in various shapes and sizes ensures that you always have a quick meal option on hand. Lentils, beans, and chickpeas, whether dried or canned, provide essential protein and fiber, and can be used in soups, stews, salads, and more.

Canned goods are invaluable for their convenience and long shelf life. Tomatoes, whether whole, diced, or in sauce form, are the foundation of countless recipes from pasta sauces to stews. Coconut milk is a key ingredient in many Asian and Caribbean dishes, adding a rich, creamy texture. Canned fish, such as tuna, salmon, and sardines, can be a quick and nutritious addition to salads, sandwiches, and pastas. Stocking a variety of broths, both vegetable and meat-based, ensures you're always prepared to make soups, risottos, and sauces.

Spices and herbs are what transform basic ingredients into flavorful dishes. A well-curated spice rack should include basics like cumin, coriander, paprika, chili powder, and turmeric. Dried herbs such as oregano, thyme, rosemary, and bay leaves are versatile and long-lasting, perfect for seasoning meats, vegetables, and soups. Don't forget about baking essentials like cinnamon, nutmeg, and vanilla extract. Quality spices and herbs can make a significant difference in your cooking, so consider sourcing them from reputable suppliers and storing them in airtight containers to maintain their potency.

Sweeteners and baking essentials go beyond just sugar. Honey, maple syrup, and molasses offer distinct flavors and can be used in both baking and cooking. Baking powder and baking soda are leavening agents necessary for many baked goods. Yeast is essential for bread making, while cocoa powder and chocolate chips are useful for both baking and creating desserts. Having a variety of nuts and seeds, such as almonds, walnuts, chia seeds, and flaxseeds, can add texture and nutritional value to baked goods and salads.

Sauces, condiments, and spreads are pantry essentials that add depth and complexity to dishes. Soy sauce, fish sauce, and Worcestershire sauce are key umami boosters. Mustards, ketchups, and mayonnaise are indispensable for sandwiches, dressings, and marinades. Nut butters like peanut and almond butter are not only great for quick snacks but also add richness to sauces and baked goods. A selection of hot sauces can cater to different heat preferences and elevate your meals with a spicy kick.

Preserved foods, such as pickles, olives, and capers, bring acidity and brininess to your cooking, cutting through rich flavors and adding complexity. Jams, jellies, and marmalades are not only for spreading on toast but can also be used in glazes, sauces, and desserts. Sun-dried tomatoes and jarred roasted red peppers offer concentrated flavors that can enhance pastas, salads, and sandwiches.

Proper organization of your pantry is crucial for efficient cooking. Group similar items together: keep baking supplies in one area, spices in another, and grains and legumes in their own section. Use clear containers for dry goods to easily see when you're running low. Label everything, especially if you transfer items from their original packaging. Regularly rotate your stock, placing newer items at the back and older items at the front to ensure nothing goes to waste.

Understanding shelf life and proper storage can prevent spoilage and food waste. Most spices lose their potency after a year, while baking powder and soda should be replaced every six months. Grains and legumes can last for up to a year if stored in a cool, dry place. Canned goods are generally safe for several years, but check for any signs of rust or bulging, which indicate spoilage. Oils can go rancid; store them in a cool, dark place and use them within a few months of opening.

Planning and maintaining a well-stocked pantry also involves regular inventory checks. Keep a running list of what you have and what you need to restock. This not only helps with grocery shopping but also ensures you're always prepared to cook a variety of meals without last-minute dashes to the store. Consider using digital tools or apps to manage your inventory and shopping lists efficiently.

Flexibility is another key aspect of a well-stocked pantry. While there are essential items that should always be on hand, tailor your pantry to suit your cooking style and dietary preferences. If you enjoy baking, prioritize a variety of flours, sugars, and baking ingredients. If you cook a lot of Asian cuisine, stock up on soy sauce, rice vinegar, and sesame oil. A pantry that reflects your culinary interests will make cooking more enjoyable and satisfying.

A thoughtfully stocked pantry is more than just a collection of ingredients; it's a strategic approach to cooking that saves time, reduces stress, and enhances creativity in the kitchen. By ensuring you have a variety of essential items on hand, you can confidently tackle any recipe, experiment with new dishes, and enjoy the process of cooking. With the right ingredients at your fingertips, your kitchen becomes a place of endless culinary possibilities. In addition to the core pantry essentials, consider incorporating a selection of international ingredients to expand your culinary repertoire and add exciting flavors to your meals. Stocking items like soy sauce, sesame oil, and miso paste can open the door to a variety of Asian dishes, while ingredients such as harissa, preserved lemons, and za'atar can bring the vibrant tastes of North African and Middle Eastern cuisine to your table.

Chapter 2

Breakfast Delights

Classic Pancakes and Waffles

Few things evoke the comfort and warmth of a leisurely morning at home like the aroma of pancakes and waffles cooking on the griddle or in the iron. These classic breakfast staples are beloved for their simplicity, versatility, and the joy they bring to both cooks and eaters alike. Mastering the art of making perfect pancakes and waffles is a rewarding pursuit that combines basic culinary skills with the opportunity for endless creativity and customization.

The foundation of any great pancake or waffle recipe lies in understanding the basic ingredients and their roles in creating the desired texture and flavor. Flour, baking powder, salt, sugar, eggs, milk, and butter are the essential components that, when combined correctly, yield fluffy, tender pancakes and crisp, golden waffles.

Flour forms the bulk of the batter, providing structure. All-purpose flour is the standard choice, but experimenting with whole wheat, buckwheat, or gluten-free flours can offer different textures and flavors. Baking powder acts as the leavening agent, giving pancakes and waffles their rise and lightness. Salt enhances the flavors, while sugar adds a touch of sweetness and helps with browning. Eggs contribute to the structure and richness, while milk provides moisture. Butter, melted and mixed into the batter, adds flavor and tenderness.

Begin by mixing the dry ingredients in one bowl and the wet ingredients in another. This method ensures that the baking powder is evenly distributed, which is crucial for proper rising. When combining the wet and dry ingredients, it's important not to overmix. Overmixing can lead to tough pancakes and waffles because it activates the gluten in the flour. Stir just until the ingredients are combined, even if there are a few lumps remaining in the batter.

For classic pancakes, heating the griddle properly is key. A medium-high heat allows the pancakes to cook through without burning the exterior. To test if the griddle is ready, sprinkle a few drops of water onto the surface; if they sizzle and evaporate almost immediately, it's time to cook. Lightly grease the griddle with butter or oil to prevent sticking and to add a bit of flavor.

Using a ladle or measuring cup, pour the batter onto the griddle in the desired size. Let the pancakes cook until bubbles form on the surface and the edges look set. This usually takes about 2-3 minutes. Flip them carefully with a spatula and cook for another 1-2 minutes on the other side until golden brown. Serve immediately with butter and maple syrup, or keep warm in a low oven while you cook the rest.

Waffles require a slightly different approach. Preheat your waffle iron according to the manufacturer's instructions. Grease it lightly to ensure the waffles release easily. Pour the batter into the center of the iron, allowing it to spread out naturally. Close the lid and cook until the waffle is golden brown and crisp. This can take anywhere from 3-5 minutes depending on your waffle iron. Remove carefully and serve with your favorite toppings.

One of the joys of pancakes and waffles is their versatility. You can customize the batter with a variety of mix-ins to suit your tastes. Fresh or frozen berries, chocolate chips, nuts, or even spices like cinnamon and nutmeg can add delightful flavors and textures. For a healthier twist, consider adding grated vegetables like zucchini or carrots, or incorporating oats or flaxseed into the batter.

Toppings offer another realm of creativity. Beyond the classic butter and maple syrup, try fresh fruit, whipped cream, yogurt, or nut butters. Savory options like fried eggs, bacon, or avocado can turn breakfast into a hearty brunch. The possibilities are endless, making pancakes and waffles suitable for any meal or occasion.

For those with dietary restrictions, there are numerous adaptations to explore. Gluten-free flours such as almond, coconut, or a gluten-free all-purpose blend can be used in place of regular flour. Non-dairy milks like almond, soy, or oat milk work well as substitutes for cow's milk. For egg-free versions, flax or chia seeds mixed with water can act as a binding agent, and coconut oil or vegan butter can replace dairy butter.

The technique of making pancakes and waffles can be refined with practice. Pay attention to the consistency of the batter; it should be thick but pourable. Too thin, and your pancakes may spread too much and be difficult to flip; too thick, and they may not cook through evenly. Adjusting the liquid or flour slightly can help achieve the perfect consistency.

Temperature control is another critical factor. If the griddle or waffle iron is too hot, the exterior will cook too quickly, leaving the inside undercooked. If it's too cool, the pancakes or waffles can turn out pale and tough. Finding the right balance may take a bit of trial and error, but it's worth the effort for the perfect result.

Keeping the batter fresh is also important. While pancake and waffle batter can be made ahead of time, it's best used within 24 hours. If you need to store it, keep it in the refrigerator and give it a gentle stir before using. For longer storage, consider freezing cooked pancakes and waffles. They reheat beautifully in the toaster or oven, providing a quick and convenient breakfast option.

Hosting a pancake or waffle breakfast can be a delightful way to bring friends and family together. Setting up a toppings bar with a variety of options allows everyone to customize their meal to their liking. Consider offering a mix of sweet and savory toppings, fresh fruit, whipped cream, nuts, and syrups. This not only adds to the enjoyment but also makes the meal interactive and fun.

In summary, mastering classic pancakes and waffles is a rewarding culinary endeavor that combines basic techniques with endless opportunities for creativity. Whether enjoyed as a simple breakfast or an elaborate brunch, these beloved dishes bring comfort and joy to any table. By understanding the essential ingredients, perfecting your technique, and exploring new flavors and toppings, you can elevate your pancake and waffle game to new heights. So, preheat your griddle or waffle iron, gather your favorite ingredients, and enjoy the delicious journey of making and sharing these timeless breakfast classics. For those who love adding a personal touch to their breakfast, consider experimenting with homemade syrups and compotes. Fresh fruit compotes can be made by simmering fruits like berries, apples, or peaches with a bit of sugar and lemon juice until they break down into a chunky sauce. These compotes can be flavored with spices like cinnamon, nutmeg, or vanilla for added depth. A homemade syrup, such as a simple vanilla or berry syrup, can be made by combining sugar, water, and your chosen flavorings in a saucepan and simmering until thickened. These homemade toppings not only enhance the flavor of your pancakes and waffles but also add a touch of homemade charm that store-bought syrups can't match.

Egg-cellent Choices: Scrambles, Omelets, and More

Eggs are one of the most versatile ingredients in the kitchen, offering countless possibilities for delicious meals at any time of day. From simple scrambles to elaborate omelets, the humble egg can be transformed into a variety of satisfying dishes with a few basic techniques and a bit of creativity. This chapter will guide you through the essentials of making perfect scrambled eggs, crafting omelets with flair, and exploring other delightful egg-based dishes.

The secret to great scrambled eggs lies in their texture and flavor. Start with fresh eggs, preferably free-range or organic, for the best taste. Crack the eggs into a bowl and whisk them thoroughly until the whites and yolks are completely combined. Adding a splash of milk or cream can make the eggs creamier, but this is optional. Season with salt and pepper, though be mindful not to overdo it, as the flavors will concentrate during cooking.

Heat a non-stick skillet over medium-low heat and add a pat of butter or a drizzle of oil. Once the butter has melted and is gently bubbling, pour in the eggs. Stir constantly with a spatula, gently folding the eggs over themselves as they cook. The key is to go low and slow; high heat can cause the eggs to become dry and rubbery. As the eggs begin to set, you can add additional ingredients such as cheese, herbs, or cooked vegetables. Continue cooking until the eggs are just set but still slightly creamy. Remove from the heat immediately, as the residual heat will continue to cook the eggs slightly.

Omelets offer a canvas for endless customization and can be as simple or elaborate as you like. The basic technique begins similarly to scrambled eggs. Whisk the eggs thoroughly and season them. Heat a non-stick skillet over medium heat and add butter or oil. Once the butter is melted, pour in the eggs and let them sit undisturbed for a moment to begin setting around the edges.

Using a spatula, gently lift the edges of the omelet, allowing the uncooked eggs to flow underneath. This helps cook the eggs evenly without overcooking the bottom. When the eggs are mostly set but still slightly wet on top, add your fillings. Classic options include cheese, ham, mushrooms, spinach, and tomatoes, but you can be as creative as you like. Fold the omelet in half or thirds, and let it cook for another minute until the cheese is melted and the fillings are heated through. Slide the omelet onto a plate and serve immediately.

Beyond scrambles and omelets, eggs can be the star of many other dishes. Frittatas, for instance, are essentially crustless quiches that can be served hot or at room temperature, making them perfect for brunches or picnics. To make a frittata, whisk together eggs, a splash of milk or cream, and your desired seasonings. Pour the mixture into a skillet with sautéed vegetables, meats, or cheeses, and cook over medium heat until the edges are set. Transfer the skillet to a preheated oven and bake until the frittata is fully set and golden brown on top. Let it cool slightly before slicing and serving.

Shakshuka, a North African and Middle Eastern dish, features eggs poached in a spicy tomato sauce. Start by sautéing onions, bell peppers, and garlic in olive oil until softened. Add tomatoes, either fresh or canned, along with spices such as cumin, paprika, and chili flakes. Simmer the sauce until thickened, then create small wells and crack the eggs into them. Cover the skillet and cook until the eggs are set to your liking. Garnish with fresh herbs like cilantro or parsley and serve with crusty bread for dipping.

For a lighter option, try an egg-white scramble or omelet. Simply separate the yolks from the whites and whisk the whites until frothy. Cook as you would a regular scramble or omelet, but be sure to add plenty of flavorful ingredients like herbs, cheese, and vegetables to compensate for the lack of richness from the yolks.

Boiled eggs are another versatile preparation, perfect for snacks, salads, or as a protein-packed addition to meals. The key to perfect boiled eggs is timing. For soft-boiled eggs with a runny yolk, cook the eggs in boiling water for about 6 minutes. For medium-boiled eggs with a slightly set yolk, aim for 8-9 minutes. For hard-boiled eggs with a fully set yolk, cook for 10-12 minutes. Once cooked, transfer the eggs to an ice bath to stop the cooking process and make peeling easier.

Poached eggs, with their delicate texture and runny yolk, are a bit trickier but well worth the effort. Bring a pot of water to a gentle simmer and add a splash of vinegar to help the eggs coagulate. Crack each egg into a small bowl or ramekin. Create a gentle whirlpool in the water with a spoon and carefully slide the egg into the center. Cook for about 3-4 minutes for a runny yolk, then remove with a slotted spoon and drain on a paper towel. Poached eggs are a classic topping for dishes like eggs Benedict or avocado toast.

For a quick and easy dish, try a breakfast burrito or sandwich. Scramble some eggs and combine them with ingredients like cooked sausage, cheese, and salsa. Wrap the mixture in a tortilla for a burrito or sandwich it between slices of bread for a hearty breakfast on the go. These portable options are perfect for busy mornings when you need something satisfying yet convenient.

Eggs can also be used in baking to create sweet treats like soufflés and custards. A cheese soufflé, for example, can make an impressive brunch dish. Start by making a béchamel sauce with butter, flour, and milk, then stir in grated cheese until melted. Whisk in egg yolks, then fold in beaten egg whites until light and airy. Pour the mixture into a buttered soufflé dish and bake until puffed and golden. Serve immediately for the best texture.

Custards, such as crème brûlée or flan, showcase the smooth, creamy texture eggs can provide. These desserts typically involve gently cooking a mixture of eggs, sugar, and cream or milk until set. The key is to cook them slowly, often in a water bath, to prevent curdling and ensure a silky result.

Incorporating eggs into your diet not only adds variety but also provides a rich source of protein, vitamins, and minerals. Eggs are particularly high in choline, which is important for brain health, and they contain antioxidants that support eye health. Whether you're looking for a quick breakfast, a hearty brunch, or an elegant dinner, the versatility of eggs makes them an indispensable ingredient in any kitchen.

The techniques and recipes outlined in this chapter are just the beginning. Experiment with different ingredients, flavors, and methods to discover your favorite ways to enjoy eggs. Whether you prefer them scrambled, poached, baked, or boiled, mastering the art of cooking eggs opens up a world of culinary possibilities. With practice and a bit of creativity, you can transform this simple ingredient into a spectacular dish that delights and satisfies. One often overlooked yet highly rewarding method of cooking eggs is baking them. Baked eggs, also known as "shirred eggs," are incredibly simple and can be prepared in individual ramekins for an elegant presentation. Begin by preheating your oven to 375°F (190°C). Grease the ramekins with butter or oil, then crack an egg into each one. You can add a splash of cream or milk over the top for added richness, and season with salt, pepper, and any herbs or spices you prefer. For a more decadent version, sprinkle grated cheese or lay a slice of smoked salmon over the eggs. Place the ramekins in a baking dish and fill the dish with hot water halfway up the sides of the ramekins to ensure even cooking. Bake for about 12-15 minutes, or until the whites are set but the yolks remain runny. Serve immediately with toast or a light salad for a sophisticated breakfast or brunch.

Healthy Smoothies and Bowls

Smoothies and bowls have become a staple in the diet of health enthusiasts and busy individuals alike, offering a quick, nutrient-dense option for any meal of the day. The beauty of these dishes lies in their versatility and the endless combinations of ingredients that can be used to tailor them to your specific nutritional needs and taste preferences. Crafting the perfect smoothie or bowl is both an art and a science, requiring a balance of macronutrients, vitamins, and minerals to ensure you are getting the most out of every sip or bite.

The foundation of any great smoothie begins with a liquid base. Water is the simplest and most calorie-free option, but you can also use milk, plant-based alternatives like almond, soy, or oat milk, or even coconut water for added flavor and hydration. Each liquid brings its own set of nutrients: dairy milk provides calcium and protein, while plant-based milks often come fortified with vitamins and minerals. Coconut water is particularly hydrating and rich in electrolytes, making it a great choice for post-workout smoothies.

Once you have your base, the next step is to add fruits and vegetables. Fresh or frozen fruits are both excellent options, with frozen fruits adding a creamy, thick texture to your smoothie without the need for ice. Berries, bananas, mangoes, and pineapples are popular choices, each bringing their own unique flavors and health benefits. Berries, for example, are packed with antioxidants, fiber, and vitamins C and K. Bananas add natural sweetness and are a good source of potassium, which helps with muscle function and maintaining proper electrolyte balance.

Vegetables, often overlooked in smoothie recipes, are a powerhouse of nutrients. Leafy greens like spinach and kale blend seamlessly into smoothies, often without altering the flavor significantly but adding a substantial amount of vitamins A, C, and K, as well as iron and fiber. For those who might be hesitant about the taste, starting with smaller amounts and gradually increasing the quantity can help your palate adjust. Other vegetables like carrots, beets, and cucumbers can also be great additions, offering their own unique vitamins and minerals along with a refreshing taste.

To ensure your smoothie is not just a blend of fruits and vegetables but a well-rounded meal, it's important to include a source of protein. This can come from various sources such as Greek yogurt, which adds creaminess and a good dose of protein and probiotics, aiding in digestion. Protein powders, whether whey, pea, hemp, or soy-based, are also convenient options that can easily be tailored to your dietary preferences and needs. Nut butters and seeds, like almond butter, chia seeds, or flaxseeds, not only contribute protein but also healthy fats, which are essential for keeping you full and satisfied.

Healthy fats are another crucial component of a balanced smoothie. Avocado, for instance, blends to a smooth consistency and provides monounsaturated fats, which are heart-healthy and good for maintaining optimal cholesterol levels. Coconut oil or MCT oil can also be added for a boost of energy, especially beneficial if you're following a ketogenic diet or looking for a quick, sustained energy source.

Sweeteners are often added to smoothies to enhance flavor, but it's important to choose natural options and use them sparingly. Honey, maple syrup, or dates can add sweetness without the blood sugar spike associated with refined sugars. However, relying on the natural sweetness of fruits is often sufficient, especially as your taste buds adjust to less sugary options over time.

Superfoods can take your smoothie to the next level, offering a concentrated dose of nutrients. Spirulina, a blue-green algae, is rich in protein, vitamins, minerals, and antioxidants. Maca powder, derived from a Peruvian root, is known for its energy-boosting properties and hormone-balancing effects. Cacao powder not only adds a rich chocolate flavor but is also packed with antioxidants and magnesium, which is important for muscle and nerve function. These additions, while not necessary, can significantly enhance the nutritional profile of your smoothie.

Smoothie bowls follow the same principles as smoothies but offer the added benefit of various toppings that can make your meal more satisfying and visually appealing. The base of a smoothie bowl is typically thicker than a smoothie, achieved by using less liquid and more frozen ingredients. Once you have your thick, creamy base, the fun begins with the toppings. Fresh fruits, granola, nuts, seeds, and even a drizzle of nut butter can add different textures and flavors, making each bite unique.

Creating a balanced smoothie bowl involves layering flavors and textures. Start with a base of blended fruits and vegetables, similar to a smoothie, but with a consistency more akin to soft-serve ice cream. Bananas and avocados are particularly useful here, providing creaminess and a neutral flavor that can be built upon with other ingredients. Once blended, pour your mixture into a bowl and start layering your toppings. Fresh berries, sliced bananas, kiwi, and mango can add vibrant colors and additional nutrients.

Granola or muesli provides a satisfying crunch and a source of whole grains, which are important for sustained energy. Opt for varieties with low sugar content or make your own to control the ingredients.

Nuts and seeds, such as almonds, walnuts, sunflower seeds, and pumpkin seeds, offer healthy fats and protein, contributing to a well-rounded meal. Chia seeds or flaxseeds sprinkled on top can add fiber and omega-3 fatty acids, which are essential for heart health and reducing inflammation.

For those looking to add a touch of indulgence, a drizzle of honey, maple syrup, or a spoonful of nut butter can enhance the flavor and make the bowl more satisfying. Coconut flakes, dark chocolate shavings, or a sprinkle of cinnamon can also add interesting flavors and textures, making your smoothie bowl not just a meal but a delightful experience.

Experimentation is key when it comes to smoothies and bowls. Don't be afraid to try new combinations of fruits, vegetables, and superfoods to discover what you enjoy most. Keep in mind the balance of macronutrients: a good mix of carbohydrates, protein, and healthy fats will keep you full and energized throughout the day.

Incorporating these nutrient-dense options into your diet can be a game-changer for your health. They offer a convenient way to consume a variety of vitamins and minerals, support digestion with fiber, and can be tailored to meet specific dietary needs or preferences. Whether you're rushing out the door in the morning or looking for a refreshing post-workout snack, smoothies and bowls provide a versatile and delicious solution to your nutritional needs. Beyond their nutritional benefits, smoothies and bowls can also be a creative outlet, allowing you to play with flavors, colors, and textures. This makes them particularly appealing for those who may struggle with incorporating a variety of fruits and vegetables into their diet. By blending and topping with a range of ingredients, you can ensure you're getting a broad spectrum of nutrients in a single, enjoyable meal.

Quick Breads and Muffins

Quick breads and muffins are beloved staples in the world of home baking, offering a delightful blend of convenience and comfort. Unlike traditional yeast breads that require time and patience for rising and kneading, quick breads and muffins rely on chemical leaveners such as baking powder and baking soda to achieve their light and fluffy texture. This makes them an ideal choice for busy households or those new to baking. Their versatility allows for a vast array of flavor combinations, making them perfect for any time of day, whether as a breakfast treat, an afternoon snack, or a dessert.

The foundation of any good quick bread or muffin begins with understanding the basic ingredients and their roles. Flour is the backbone, providing structure. All-purpose flour is the most commonly used, but whole wheat flour can add a nutty flavor and additional fiber. For those with gluten sensitivities, gluten-free flours like almond flour or oat flour can be used, though they may require adjustments in liquid ingredients or the addition of binders like xanthan gum to achieve the desired texture.

Leavening agents, such as baking powder and baking soda, are crucial for the rise and fluffiness of your baked goods. Baking powder contains both an acid and a base, which react when mixed with liquid and heat to produce carbon dioxide bubbles, causing the dough to rise. Baking soda, on the other hand, requires an acidic ingredient like buttermilk, yogurt, or lemon juice to activate it. Understanding the correct ratios and combinations of these leaveners is key to avoiding dense or overly crumbly results.

Sweeteners not only provide sweetness but also contribute to the moisture and tenderness of quick breads and muffins. Granulated sugar is standard, but brown sugar, honey, maple syrup, or even mashed fruits like bananas or applesauce can be used to add depth of flavor and moisture. Each sweetener brings its own unique characteristics: brown sugar adds a rich, caramel flavor and extra moisture, while honey and maple syrup infuse a subtle complexity and help keep the bread or muffins soft.

Fat is another essential component, providing richness and aiding in moisture retention. Butter is a classic choice, imparting a rich flavor and tender crumb. However, oil, whether vegetable, coconut, or olive, can also be used and often results in a moister end product. For a healthier twist, consider using mashed avocado or Greek yogurt, which add healthy fats and additional nutrients without sacrificing texture.

Eggs play a crucial role in binding the ingredients together and adding structure. They also contribute to the richness and color of the baked goods. For those who follow a vegan diet or have egg allergies, substitutes like flax eggs, chia eggs, or commercial egg replacers can be used. The general rule of thumb is to mix one tablespoon of ground flaxseed or chia seeds with three tablespoons of water to replace one egg.

Liquid ingredients, typically milk or a non-dairy alternative, are necessary to hydrate the dry ingredients and create a smooth batter. Buttermilk is a popular choice for its tangy flavor and ability to react with baking soda, enhancing the leavening process. For a dairy-free option, almond milk, soy milk, or oat milk can be used, each bringing its own subtle flavor to the mix.

Once you have a grasp of these basic ingredients and their functions, you can begin to experiment with flavors and add-ins. Fruits, nuts, spices, and extracts can transform a simple quick bread or muffin into a gourmet delight. Bananas, blueberries, and zucchini are popular choices, adding both flavor and moisture. Nuts like walnuts, pecans, or almonds provide a satisfying crunch and additional nutrients. Spices such as cinnamon, nutmeg, and cardamom can elevate the flavor profile, while extracts like vanilla or almond add depth and complexity.

The method of mixing is also crucial in achieving the perfect texture. Overmixing the batter can result in tough, dense baked goods due to the overdevelopment of gluten. It's important to mix the dry and wet ingredients separately before combining them, and then gently fold the wet mixture into the dry ingredients until just combined. Lumps in the batter are perfectly acceptable and often desirable, as they ensure a tender crumb.

Baking time and temperature are also critical factors. Quick breads and muffins are typically baked at a higher temperature, around 350 to 375 degrees Fahrenheit, to achieve a golden brown crust and a moist interior. Muffins usually take about 15-20 minutes, while quick breads can take anywhere from 40-60 minutes, depending on the size and density of the loaf. Always check for doneness by inserting a toothpick into the center; it should come out clean or with just a few crumbs clinging to it.

One of the joys of baking quick breads and muffins is the ability to customize them to suit dietary needs or personal preferences. For a healthier option, consider reducing the amount of sugar or using natural sweeteners like honey or maple syrup. Whole grain flours can be used in place of all-purpose flour to increase fiber content. Adding ingredients like flaxseed, chia seeds, or protein powder can boost the nutritional value.

Moreover, these baked goods can be made ahead and stored for later use, making them perfect for meal prep. Quick breads can be wrapped tightly and stored at room temperature for up to three days, or frozen for up to three months. Muffins can be kept in an airtight container at room temperature for a few days, or frozen individually for a convenient grab-and-go option.

Incorporating seasonal ingredients is another way to enhance the flavor and variety of your quick breads and muffins. In the fall, pumpkin and apple are popular choices, often paired with warm spices like cinnamon and cloves. Winter might see the addition of cranberries and citrus, while spring and summer are perfect for berries, peaches, and zucchini. Using fresh, in-season produce not only enhances the flavor but also supports local farmers and reduces your carbon footprint.

For those looking to add a bit of indulgence, incorporating chocolate chips, a swirl of Nutella, or a streusel topping can transform a simple quick bread or muffin into a decadent treat. These additions are perfect for special occasions or when you simply want to treat yourself.

Quick breads and muffins also make excellent gifts. A beautifully wrapped loaf or a basket of muffins can be a thoughtful and delicious present for friends, family, or neighbors. Personalizing the flavors to suit the recipient's tastes or dietary preferences shows extra care and consideration.

In conclusion, quick breads and muffins are a versatile, convenient, and delightful addition to any home baker's repertoire. With a basic understanding of the ingredients and techniques, the possibilities are endless. Whether you're seeking a healthy breakfast option, a satisfying snack, or a sweet treat, these baked goods offer something for everyone. By experimenting with different flavors, add-ins, and dietary adaptations, you can create a wide variety of delicious breads and muffins that are sure to please any palate. Sharing quick breads and muffins with others can foster a sense of community and connection. Hosting a baking day with friends or family allows you to bond over the shared experience of creating something delicious together. This can be an especially fun activity with children, teaching them valuable kitchen skills and inspiring a love for baking. Letting them mix the batter, measure ingredients, or sprinkle toppings can make the process engaging and educational.

Family Brunch Favorites

Family brunches offer a special opportunity to gather loved ones and share a meal filled with warmth and conversation. These occasions call for dishes that are not only delicious but also easy to prepare, allowing you to spend more time with your family and less time in the kitchen. The key to a successful family brunch lies in balancing flavors, textures, and dietary preferences, ensuring there's something for everyone to enjoy.

A brunch staple that never fails to impress is the classic quiche. This versatile dish can be customized to suit various tastes and dietary needs. A quiche begins with a buttery, flaky crust, which can be made from scratch or bought pre-made for convenience. The filling typically consists of eggs, cream, and cheese, combined with a variety of vegetables, meats, or seafood. For a classic Lorraine, use bacon and Gruyère cheese. A vegetarian option could include spinach, mushrooms, and feta. The quiche can be prepared the night before and simply baked in the morning, making it a stress-free addition to your brunch table.

Another crowd-pleaser is the breakfast casserole. This dish is perfect for feeding a large group and can be tailored to suit different preferences. A base of cubed bread soaked in an egg mixture provides a hearty foundation. Add-ins such as sausage, ham, cheese, and vegetables make it a complete meal. Consider a southwestern twist with chorizo, bell peppers, and pepper jack cheese, or an Italian version with Italian sausage, sun-dried tomatoes, and mozzarella. Like quiche, breakfast casseroles can be assembled the night before and baked in the morning, allowing you more time to relax and enjoy your company.

Pancakes and waffles are perennial favorites that can be made extra special with a few simple additions. For pancakes, consider adding blueberries, chocolate chips, or a touch of cinnamon to the batter. Serve them with a variety of toppings like fresh fruit, whipped cream, and pure maple syrup. Waffles can be equally delightful, especially when made with a yeast batter, which gives them a light and crispy texture. Offer a selection of toppings such as berries, nuts, and flavored syrups to let each guest customize their plate.

For a lighter option, a yogurt parfait bar is both healthy and visually appealing. Set out bowls of Greek yogurt, granola, and an assortment of fresh fruit such as berries, sliced bananas, and kiwi. Add some honey, nuts, and seeds for extra flavor and crunch. This option not only caters to health-conscious guests but also adds a beautiful array of colors to your brunch spread.

Egg dishes are a cornerstone of any brunch menu, and there are countless ways to prepare them. Scrambled eggs are a simple and classic choice, but you can elevate them by adding ingredients like smoked salmon, cream cheese, and chives. Another elegant option is Eggs Benedict, featuring poached eggs and Canadian bacon on an English muffin, topped with rich hollandaise sauce. For a more casual approach, consider a frittata, which is similar to a quiche but without the crust. It's easy to customize with your favorite fillings and can be served hot or at room temperature.

French toast is another beloved brunch dish that can be easily customized. Use thick slices of brioche or challah bread for a rich, custard-like texture. For a decadent twist, stuff the bread with cream cheese and fresh berries before dipping it in the egg mixture. Serve with a dusting of powdered sugar, a drizzle of maple syrup, and a side of fresh fruit.

No brunch is complete without a selection of beverages. Freshly squeezed orange juice, coffee, and tea are must-haves. For a special touch, consider making a batch of mimosas or a pitcher of Bloody Marys. A fruit-infused water with slices of cucumber, lemon, and mint is a refreshing non-alcoholic option that's both hydrating and visually appealing.

Baked goods add a comforting and sweet element to the brunch table. Muffins, scones, and pastries can be prepared in advance and served with butter and preserves. Blueberry muffins, chocolate chip scones, and flaky croissants are always popular choices. For a more indulgent treat, consider cinnamon rolls with cream cheese frosting, which can be prepped the night before and baked fresh in the morning.

Salads may not be the first thing that comes to mind for brunch, but they can provide a fresh and vibrant contrast to heavier dishes. A simple green salad with mixed greens, cherry tomatoes, and a light vinaigrette is a refreshing addition. For something more substantial, consider a grain salad with quinoa, roasted vegetables, and a lemon-tahini dressing. A fruit salad with a mix of seasonal fruits, mint, and a squeeze of lime is a sweet and tangy way to cleanse the palate.

For those who enjoy savory flavors, consider adding a charcuterie board to your brunch spread. A selection of cured meats, cheeses, olives, and pickles can provide a satisfying and sophisticated element. Add some crusty bread or crackers, and perhaps a few spreads like hummus or tapenade, to round out the offering.

In addition to the main dishes, side items like roasted potatoes or a vegetable medley can complement the meal. Roasted potatoes, seasoned with herbs and garlic, are always a hit. A medley of roasted or sautéed vegetables, such as bell peppers, zucchini, and asparagus, adds color and nutrition to the table.

For a touch of whimsy and fun, consider incorporating a theme into your brunch. A Mediterranean brunch could feature dishes like shakshuka, a tomato and egg dish, alongside hummus and pita. A Southern-style brunch might include biscuits and gravy, shrimp and grits, and sweet tea. Themes can provide inspiration for your menu and make the event even more memorable.

As you plan your family brunch, remember that the goal is to create a warm and inviting atmosphere where everyone feels welcome and relaxed. Setting a pretty table with fresh flowers, colorful napkins, and elegant dishware can enhance the experience. Playing soft background music can also set a pleasant tone without overpowering conversation.

Finally, involve your family in the preparation. Assign tasks to different members, whether it's setting the table, mixing batter, or arranging fruit platters. This not only lightens the load but also makes the brunch a collaborative event where everyone contributes.

Family brunches are more than just a meal; they are an opportunity to create lasting memories. By preparing a variety of dishes that cater to different tastes and dietary needs, you can ensure that everyone leaves the table satisfied and happy. Embrace the joy of cooking and sharing food with your loved ones, and your family brunch will surely become a cherished tradition. One aspect of family brunch that often goes overlooked is the importance of planning and timing. Successful brunches hinge not just on the quality of the food, but also on the seamless flow from preparation to dining. Begin by mapping out your menu and creating a detailed timeline. Identify which dishes can be made ahead of time and which need to be prepared on the day of the brunch. This will help you manage your time effectively and reduce last-minute stress.

Chapter 3

Appetizers and Snacks

Dips and Spreads

Dips and spreads are the unsung heroes of casual entertaining. They're versatile, easy to prepare, and can elevate any gathering, from a simple family get-together to a grand holiday feast. With a few basic ingredients and a bit of creativity, you can whip up a variety of dips and spreads that will delight and impress your guests. Understanding the balance of flavors and textures is key to creating dips and spreads that will become the stars of your appetizer table.

One of the most beloved and versatile dips is hummus. Traditionally made from chickpeas, tahini, lemon juice, garlic, and olive oil, hummus is a creamy, savory dip that pairs well with almost everything. Start by blending cooked chickpeas with tahini in a food processor, then add fresh lemon juice, minced garlic, and a good quality olive oil. Season with salt to taste and, if desired, a pinch of cumin for a touch of warmth. The beauty of hummus lies in its adaptability. You can infuse it with various flavors by adding ingredients like roasted red peppers, sun-dried tomatoes, or even fresh herbs like basil and cilantro. Serve it with warm pita bread, fresh vegetables, or use it as a spread in sandwiches.

Guacamole is another crowd-pleaser that never goes out of style. This creamy, zesty dip is made from ripe avocados, lime juice, cilantro, and diced onions. Start by mashing the avocados to your desired consistency—some prefer it smooth, while others like it chunky. Mix in freshly squeezed lime juice, which not only adds flavor but also prevents the avocados from browning. Finely chopped cilantro and onions add a fresh, aromatic quality. Season with salt, and for a bit of heat, add diced jalapeños. You can also experiment with variations by incorporating ingredients like diced tomatoes, garlic, or even fruit like mango for a sweet twist. Serve guacamole with tortilla chips or as a topping for tacos and nachos.

For a dip that combines creaminess with a bit of tang, consider making tzatziki. This Greek dip made from yogurt, cucumber, garlic, and dill is refreshing and light. Begin by grating a cucumber and squeezing out the excess moisture. Mix the cucumber with Greek yogurt, minced garlic, fresh dill, and a splash of lemon juice. Drizzle with olive oil and season with salt to taste. The result is a cool, creamy dip that pairs wonderfully with grilled meats, vegetables, or simply with pita bread. Tzatziki is also excellent as a spread in wraps and sandwiches, adding a bright, tangy note.

Spinach and artichoke dip is a rich, savory option that is always a hit at parties. To make this dip, start by sautéing spinach and artichoke hearts until tender. Mix them with cream cheese, sour cream, mayonnaise, and a blend of grated cheeses such as Parmesan and mozzarella. Season with garlic, salt, and pepper, then bake until bubbly and golden. This warm, cheesy dip is perfect with crusty bread, crackers, or fresh vegetables. For a lighter version, you can substitute Greek yogurt for the sour cream and mayonnaise, or use light cream cheese.

Pesto is a versatile spread that can be used in countless ways. The classic Genovese pesto is made from fresh basil, pine nuts, Parmesan cheese, garlic, and olive oil. Blend these ingredients until smooth, adding the olive oil gradually to achieve the desired consistency. Pesto can be used as a dip for bread, a spread for sandwiches, or a topping for pasta. You can also experiment with different greens and nuts to create variations, such as arugula and walnut pesto or kale and almond pesto. Each version brings its own unique flavor profile, making pesto a constantly evolving addition to your culinary repertoire.

For a sweet option, consider a fruit-based spread like apple butter. This spread is made by cooking down apples with sugar and spices until they reach a thick, spreadable consistency. Begin by peeling, coring, and slicing a variety of apples. Cook them with a bit of water, sugar, cinnamon, and a pinch of cloves until the apples are very soft. Blend until smooth, then continue to cook on low heat until the mixture thickens to a buttery consistency. Apple butter is delicious spread on toast, biscuits, or as a filling for pastries. It also makes a lovely gift when jarred and tied with a ribbon.

Baba ghanoush is a smoky, creamy dip made from roasted eggplants. To make it, begin by roasting whole eggplants until the skin is charred and the flesh is tender. Scoop out the flesh and blend it with tahini, lemon juice, garlic, and olive oil. Season with salt and a bit of cumin for added depth. The smoky flavor of the eggplant combined with the creamy tahini and bright lemon juice makes baba ghanoush a unique and flavorful dip. Serve it with pita bread, fresh vegetables, or use it as a spread in wraps and sandwiches.

A cheese-based spread like pimento cheese can add a Southern flair to your appetizer table. This spread is made from grated cheddar cheese, mayonnaise, and diced pimentos. Mix these ingredients together until well combined, then season with a bit of garlic powder, onion powder, and a dash of hot sauce for a slight kick. Pimento cheese is delicious spread on crackers, used as a filling for sandwiches, or even melted on top of burgers. It's a versatile and flavorful spread that is sure to be a hit.

Another simple yet elegant option is a whipped ricotta spread. Ricotta cheese, when whipped with a bit of olive oil, salt, and pepper, becomes incredibly smooth and creamy. You can flavor it with herbs like thyme or rosemary, or add a bit of honey for a sweet variation. Whipped ricotta can be spread on toast, used as a dip for vegetables, or served alongside fruit for a light and refreshing appetizer.

For something a bit more exotic, try making muhammara, a Middle Eastern dip made from roasted red peppers, walnuts, and pomegranate molasses. Blend these ingredients together with a bit of garlic, lemon juice, and olive oil until smooth. The result is a rich, flavorful dip with a balance of sweetness, nuttiness, and tanginess. Muhammara is excellent with pita bread, fresh vegetables, or as a spread in sandwiches.

Creating a variety of dips and spreads not only adds flavor and interest to your dining table but also allows for a range of textures and tastes that can cater to different preferences. Whether you're hosting a large gathering or enjoying a quiet evening with family, these dips and spreads can transform simple ingredients into delightful dishes that everyone will enjoy. Experiment with different combinations and ingredients to find your favorites, and don't be afraid to put your own twist on classic recipes. With a bit of creativity and a few basic techniques, you can create a spread that is both delicious and impressive. In addition to the classic dips and spreads mentioned, consider incorporating international flavors into your repertoire to surprise and delight your guests. Salsa, for instance, offers a vibrant and fresh option that can be customized to suit different palates. A traditional tomato salsa combines ripe tomatoes, onions, cilantro, jalapeños, lime juice, and salt. For a twist, try a mango salsa by substituting tomatoes with diced mangoes and adding red bell peppers for crunch. Pineapple salsa, with its sweet and tangy profile, pairs beautifully with grilled meats and seafood.

Finger Foods and Small Bites

Finger foods and small bites are the backbone of any successful gathering, offering guests a variety of flavors and textures in easy-to-eat portions. These miniature delights not only encourage mingling and conversation but also allow for creativity in presentation and ingredient combinations. Crafting the perfect finger foods involves balancing taste, appearance, and practicality, ensuring each bite is both memorable and manageable.

One of the most beloved finger foods is the classic canapé, a small, decorative hors d'oeuvre typically consisting of a base, a flavorful topping, and a garnish. The base can range from a slice of baguette or cracker to more inventive options like cucumber rounds or endive leaves. Toppings are where creativity shines—think smoked salmon with cream cheese, roasted vegetables with goat cheese, or even a dollop of spicy hummus. Garnishes like fresh herbs, microgreens, or a drizzle of balsamic reduction can elevate the visual appeal and add a burst of fresh flavor.

Sliders, the tiny versions of burgers, have become a popular choice for parties and events. These miniature sandwiches are endlessly customizable, catering to both meat lovers and vegetarians. Classic beef sliders with cheddar and pickles can sit alongside more adventurous options like pulled pork with coleslaw or portobello mushrooms with Swiss cheese and caramelized onions. The key to a good slider is ensuring the bun-to-filling ratio is balanced, preventing the sandwich from becoming too bulky or too dry.

Spring rolls are another versatile option, offering a refreshing, crunchy bite that can be filled with a variety of ingredients. Traditional Vietnamese spring rolls are filled with shrimp, vermicelli noodles, fresh herbs, and vegetables, all wrapped in rice paper. For a twist, consider using smoked salmon, avocado, and cucumber, or even a sweet version with fruits like mango and strawberries. Accompanying dipping sauces, such as peanut sauce, hoisin sauce, or a tangy soy-based dip, add layers of flavor and provide an interactive element for guests.

Mini quiches and tarts are perfect for adding a touch of elegance to your appetizer spread. These bite-sized pastries can be filled with a wide range of savory ingredients, from classic combinations like spinach and feta to more gourmet options like caramelized onion and Gruyère or smoked salmon and dill. Using pre-made pastry shells can save time, allowing you to focus on creating flavorful fillings. These small bites are not only delicious but also visually appealing, often featuring vibrant colors and intricate designs.

Skewers, or kebabs, offer a practical and visually appealing way to serve a variety of ingredients. Whether you choose to grill, bake, or serve them cold, skewers can be tailored to suit any theme or dietary preference. Grilled chicken skewers with a tangy teriyaki glaze, shrimp and pineapple skewers, or caprese skewers with cherry tomatoes, mozzarella balls, and basil are all crowd-pleasers. The key to successful skewers is ensuring the ingredients are cut to a similar size for even cooking and easy eating.

Stuffed vegetables provide a healthy and colorful addition to your finger food selection. Cherry tomatoes, mini bell peppers, and mushrooms can be hollowed out and filled with a variety of mixtures. Consider stuffing cherry tomatoes with a blend of mozzarella, basil, and balsamic glaze, or filling mini bell peppers with a quinoa and black bean salad. Mushrooms can be stuffed with a savory mixture of cream cheese, garlic, and herbs, then baked until golden and tender. These bite-sized treats are not only tasty but also add a burst of color to your table.

Deviled eggs are a timeless favorite, offering a creamy, tangy bite that can be customized with various toppings. The classic recipe involves hard-boiled eggs, halved and filled with a mixture of the yolks, mayonnaise, mustard, and a touch of vinegar. For a modern twist, consider adding ingredients like smoked salmon, avocado, or even sriracha for a spicy kick. Garnishing with chives, paprika, or microgreens can add a finishing touch that enhances both flavor and presentation.

Empanadas, small hand-held pastries filled with savory or sweet fillings, are perfect for a more substantial finger food option. Traditional fillings include seasoned ground beef, chicken, or cheese, but you can also experiment with more unique combinations like spinach and ricotta or even a dessert version with apples and cinnamon. The dough can be made from scratch or purchased pre-made to save time. Baking rather than frying empanadas can make them a bit healthier while still ensuring a crispy, golden exterior.

Miniature versions of traditional dishes can also be a hit at gatherings. Think mini meatballs served with a tangy dipping sauce, small cups of soup with a tiny spoon, or even bite-sized portions of pasta served in individual cups. These miniaturized dishes allow guests to enjoy a variety of flavors without committing to a full serving, making them ideal for tasting and sharing.

When planning your finger foods and small bites, consider the overall balance and variety. Aim for a mix of hot and cold options, and ensure there are choices that cater to different dietary needs, such as vegetarian, gluten-free, and dairy-free. Presentation is also crucial—arranging your bites on platters with garnishes and decorative elements can make a significant impact.

To create a cohesive and attractive presentation, think about the colors and textures of your foods. Using a variety of vibrant, fresh ingredients can make your spread visually appealing. Incorporating different textures, such as crunchy, creamy, and chewy, keeps the eating experience interesting. Additionally, using attractive serving ware, like wooden boards, colorful plates, or elegant trays, can enhance the overall aesthetic.

Timing is another important factor when preparing finger foods. Many items can be made ahead of time, allowing you to enjoy your event without being stuck in the kitchen. Cold items like dips, spreads, and certain canapés can often be prepared hours in advance and kept in the refrigerator until needed. Hot items can be prepped and then quickly reheated or cooked just before serving.

Consider the ease of eating when planning your small bites. Foods that are too messy or difficult to handle may detract from the enjoyment. Using toothpicks, skewers, or small cups can help manage this issue. Additionally, providing plenty of napkins and small plates ensures guests can enjoy the food comfortably.

Finger foods and small bites offer a wonderful opportunity to explore different cuisines and flavor profiles. Experimenting with international dishes, such as Spanish tapas, Italian antipasti, or Middle

Eastern mezze, can bring a global flair to your event. Each culture offers unique small dishes that can be adapted to suit your guests' tastes.

Incorporating seasonal ingredients can also elevate your finger foods. Fresh, local produce not only tastes better but also adds a touch of sophistication and thoughtfulness to your offerings. In the summer, consider using fresh berries, tomatoes, and herbs, while in the fall, root vegetables and squashes can take center stage.

Ultimately, the goal of finger foods and small bites is to create an enjoyable, interactive dining experience. By offering a variety of flavors, textures, and presentations, you can ensure your guests have a memorable time, savoring each delightful bite. Whether you're hosting a casual gathering or a formal event, these miniature morsels are sure to impress and satisfy. Attention to detail in the execution of your finger foods can significantly enhance the overall experience for your guests. One often overlooked aspect is the harmony of flavors within each bite. Balancing sweet, salty, sour, and umami elements can create a more complex and satisfying taste profile. For instance, a crostini topped with blue cheese and fig jam offers a perfect blend of creamy, tangy, and sweet flavors. Similarly, pairing a spicy shrimp skewer with a cool, creamy avocado dip can create a delightful contrast that excites the palate.

Savory Pastries and Puffs

Savory pastries and puffs are a delightful addition to any culinary repertoire, offering a satisfying blend of textures and flavors that can please even the most discerning palates. These versatile treats can be served as appetizers, snacks, or even main courses, depending on their size and filling. Mastering the art of creating savory pastries involves understanding the fundamentals of dough preparation, filling selection, and baking techniques, ensuring each bite is a perfect harmony of crispiness and savory goodness.

One of the most popular types of savory pastries is the classic puff pastry. This light, flaky dough is created by layering butter between sheets of dough, then folding and rolling it multiple times to create thin, alternating layers. The result is a pastry that puffs up beautifully in the oven, creating a crisp exterior and tender interior. While making puff pastry from scratch can be a labor-intensive process, the results are well worth the effort. For those short on time, high-quality store-bought puff pastry can be a convenient and effective alternative.

Empanadas are another beloved savory pastry, originating from Latin America and Spain. These hand-held pies are typically filled with seasoned meats, vegetables, and sometimes cheese, all encased in a tender, flaky dough. The dough for empanadas can vary from region to region, but it generally consists of flour, fat (such as butter or lard), and a liquid (like water or milk). The key to a successful empanada is ensuring the filling is flavorful and not too wet, which can cause the pastry to become soggy.

Popular fillings include ground beef with onions, olives, and hard-boiled eggs, or a vegetarian option with spinach, cheese, and spices.

Another crowd-pleaser is the sausage roll, a staple in British cuisine that has gained popularity worldwide. These savory pastries feature seasoned sausage meat wrapped in puff pastry and baked until golden brown. The combination of the rich, savory sausage and the buttery, flaky pastry makes for an irresistible treat. Variations of the sausage roll can include adding herbs, spices, or even incorporating vegetables into the sausage mixture for added flavor and nutrition. Miniature versions of sausage rolls make excellent appetizers or party snacks, while larger versions can be served as a main course.

Quiches and tarts are also prominent members of the savory pastry family, offering a wide range of filling possibilities. A quiche typically consists of a pastry crust filled with a savory custard made from eggs and cream, along with various ingredients such as cheese, vegetables, and meats. The classic Quiche Lorraine, with its filling of bacon and cheese, is a timeless favorite. Tarts, on the other hand, can have either a shortcrust or puff pastry base and are often filled with ingredients like caramelized onions, goat cheese, and roasted vegetables. Both quiches and tarts are versatile and can be served hot or cold, making them ideal for brunches, picnics, or casual dinners.

Spanakopita is a Greek savory pastry that showcases the delightful combination of spinach and feta cheese wrapped in layers of phyllo dough. Phyllo dough, much like puff pastry, is known for its thin, crisp layers, but it requires a different technique. The dough is brushed with melted butter or oil between each layer to achieve its characteristic flakiness. Spanakopita can be made as a large pie or as individual triangles, both of which are delicious and visually appealing. The filling often includes spinach, feta, onions, and herbs like dill or parsley, creating a flavorful and aromatic pastry.

Savory scones and biscuits also deserve a mention in the realm of savory pastries. These quick breads are typically made with flour, butter, and a leavening agent like baking powder. The dough is mixed until just combined, then baked to produce a tender, flaky texture. Adding ingredients such as cheese, herbs, and cooked bacon or ham can transform a plain scone or biscuit into a savory delight. They are perfect for breakfast, brunch, or as an accompaniment to soups and stews.

Creating savory pastries also involves experimenting with different fillings and flavor combinations. For example, a savory galette, which is a free-form tart, can be filled with roasted vegetables, cheese, and fresh herbs. The rustic appearance of a galette adds to its charm and makes it a visually appealing dish. Another option is to make savory turnovers, which are similar to empanadas but can feature a variety of international flavors. Think of a curry-spiced chicken filling or a Mediterranean-inspired mixture with olives, sun-dried tomatoes, and feta.

When working with savory pastries, it's important to consider the balance of flavors and textures. A good filling should be well-seasoned but not overpowering, allowing the delicate pastry to shine. Incorporating a mix of textures, such as combining creamy cheeses with crunchy vegetables or nuts, can make the pastry more interesting and enjoyable to eat. Additionally, using high-quality ingredients, such as fresh herbs, premium cheeses, and organic vegetables, can elevate the overall taste and presentation of the dish.

Baking techniques play a crucial role in achieving the perfect savory pastry. Ensuring the pastry is well-chilled before baking can help prevent it from shrinking or becoming too soft. Using a hot oven temperature can promote even puffing and browning, resulting in a crisp, flaky texture. It's also important to avoid over-filling the pastries, as this can cause them to burst or become soggy during baking. For larger pastries like pies or tarts, using a pie shield or covering the edges with foil can prevent the crust from over-browning while the filling cooks through.

Serving savory pastries can be as simple or as elaborate as you like. They can be presented on a beautiful platter with garnishes like fresh herbs or edible flowers, or served with complementary dips and sauces. For example, a yogurt-based dip with herbs and lemon can be a refreshing accompaniment to spanakopita, while a tangy tomato chutney pairs well with sausage rolls. Offering a variety of savory pastries at a gathering can provide guests with an array of flavors and textures to enjoy.

Savory pastries and puffs are a testament to the artistry and versatility of baking. Whether you're making a classic quiche, a batch of empanadas, or experimenting with new flavor combinations, these delicious treats are sure to impress. By mastering the techniques and understanding the balance of flavors, you can create savory pastries that are not only visually stunning but also incredibly satisfying to eat. They are perfect for any occasion, from casual family dinners to elegant parties, and they offer endless possibilities for creativity and enjoyment in the kitchen. Savory pastries and puffs also allow for cultural exploration through their diverse origins and unique preparations. For instance, samosas are a popular Indian savory pastry, often filled with spiced potatoes, peas, and sometimes meat. These triangular pastries are typically deep-fried to achieve a crispy exterior, though they can also be baked for a lighter version. The combination of spices like cumin, coriander, and garam masala in the filling provides a burst of flavor that is both aromatic and satisfying. Serving samosas with chutneys, such as tamarind or mint, adds an extra layer of taste and enhances the overall experience.

Healthy Snack Ideas

Healthy snacks play a crucial role in maintaining energy levels and ensuring a balanced diet throughout the day. They serve as mini-meals that bridge the gap between main meals, preventing overeating and keeping blood sugar levels stable. For those looking to adopt healthier eating habits, incorporating nutritious snacks into their daily routine is an excellent starting point. Here, we explore a variety of wholesome snack ideas that are both delicious and easy to prepare, making the journey to better health an enjoyable one.

Fruits and vegetables are among the best snacks available due to their natural vitamins, minerals, and fiber content. They are low in calories and high in nutrients, making them perfect for those aiming to eat healthily. For instance, apple slices paired with a small serving of almond butter provide a satisfying combination of sweetness and protein. Similarly, carrot sticks with hummus offer a crunchy, savory option that is rich in fiber and protein. Preparing a colorful vegetable platter with bell peppers, cherry tomatoes, cucumbers, and a homemade Greek yogurt dip not only looks appealing but also provides a variety of nutrients in one snack.

Nuts and seeds are another excellent choice for healthy snacking. They are packed with healthy fats, protein, and essential nutrients. A handful of mixed nuts, such as almonds, walnuts, and cashews, can be both satisfying and nutritious. Seeds, like pumpkin and sunflower seeds, are also great options. For a bit of variety, consider making your own trail mix by combining nuts, seeds, and dried fruits. This way, you can control the ingredients and avoid added sugars and unhealthy oils often found in store-bought versions. Just be mindful of portion sizes, as nuts and seeds are calorie-dense.

Whole grains are a cornerstone of a healthy diet and can be easily incorporated into snacks. Whole grain crackers or rice cakes topped with avocado slices and a sprinkle of sea salt create a delightful, nutrient-rich snack. Another option is to prepare a batch of homemade granola bars using oats, honey, and a mix of nuts and dried fruits. These bars can be customized to your taste and provide a portable, energy-boosting snack. Popcorn, when air-popped and lightly seasoned, is a whole grain snack that is low in calories but high in fiber, making it a great choice for those looking to curb their appetite between meals.

Dairy products, particularly those low in fat, can also be part of a healthy snacking regimen. Greek yogurt, for example, is high in protein and can be enhanced with fresh fruits, a drizzle of honey, or a sprinkle of granola for added texture and flavor. Cottage cheese paired with pineapple chunks or cucumber slices offers a refreshing, protein-packed snack. Cheese sticks or slices of hard cheese, such as cheddar or mozzarella, can be paired with whole grain crackers or apple slices for a balanced, satisfying treat. Choosing low-fat or fat-free dairy options can help manage calorie intake while still providing essential nutrients like calcium and vitamin D.

Legumes, such as beans and lentils, are not only nutritious but also versatile for snacking. Roasted chickpeas, seasoned with spices like paprika or garlic powder, make for a crunchy, protein-rich snack. Edamame, lightly steamed and sprinkled with sea salt, is another excellent option that is high in protein and fiber. Preparing a bean dip, such as a black bean dip or a classic hummus made from chickpeas, can provide a tasty and nutritious accompaniment to vegetable sticks or whole grain crackers.

Smoothies are a fantastic way to combine multiple healthy ingredients into one convenient snack. By blending a variety of fruits, vegetables, and a protein source like Greek yogurt or protein powder, you can create a nutrient-dense drink that is both delicious and filling. Adding leafy greens such as spinach or kale, along with a banana and some berries, results in a smoothie that is rich in vitamins, minerals, and antioxidants. For an extra boost, consider adding chia seeds, flaxseeds, or a spoonful of nut butter.

Hard-boiled eggs are a simple yet nutritious snack that is easy to prepare in advance. They are rich in protein and healthy fats, making them a filling option. You can enjoy them plain or with a sprinkle of seasoning, such as paprika or everything bagel seasoning, for added flavor. Pairing a hard-boiled egg with a piece of fruit or some vegetable sticks can create a balanced snack that keeps you satisfied until your next meal.

For those with a sweet tooth, there are plenty of healthy snack options that can satisfy cravings without compromising nutrition. Fresh fruit is nature's candy and comes in a variety of flavors and textures. Berries, such as strawberries, blueberries, and raspberries, are particularly high in antioxidants and can be enjoyed on their own or mixed into yogurt or oatmeal. Making a fruit salad with a mix of your favorite fruits, perhaps with a squeeze of lime juice and a handful of mint leaves, can be a refreshing and naturally sweet snack.

Dark chocolate, when consumed in moderation, can be part of a healthy diet. Choosing dark chocolate with a high cocoa content (70% or higher) ensures that you are getting more antioxidants and less sugar. Pairing a small piece of dark chocolate with a handful of nuts can provide a satisfying mix of sweet and savory flavors, along with a boost of healthy fats and protein.

Hydration is an often-overlooked aspect of healthy snacking. Sometimes what we interpret as hunger is actually thirst. Drinking plenty of water throughout the day is essential for overall health. Infusing water with slices of citrus fruits, cucumber, or berries can make it more appealing and encourage regular consumption. Herbal teas, whether hot or iced, can also be a flavorful way to stay hydrated without added sugars or calories.

Planning and preparation are key to maintaining a healthy snacking routine. Setting aside time each week to prepare snacks can ensure that you always have nutritious options available. Pre-cutting vegetables, portioning out nuts and seeds, and preparing dips or spreads can make healthy snacking convenient and accessible. Keeping these snacks in easy-to-reach places, such as in the front of the refrigerator or in a designated snack drawer, can help you make better choices when hunger strikes.

Incorporating a variety of textures, flavors, and food groups into your snacks can also make healthy eating more enjoyable and sustainable. Mixing crunchy, creamy, sweet, and savory elements keeps your taste buds engaged and can prevent boredom. Exploring different cuisines and ingredients can introduce new and exciting flavors into your diet, making healthy snacking a culinary adventure.

Listening to your body's hunger and fullness cues is crucial for mindful snacking. Eating slowly and savoring each bite can help you recognize when you are satisfied, preventing overeating. It's important to snack because you're genuinely hungry, not out of boredom or habit. By paying attention to how different snacks make you feel, you can identify which options provide lasting energy and which might leave you feeling unsatisfied.

Healthy snacking is an integral part of a balanced diet, offering numerous benefits from sustaining energy levels to enhancing nutrient intake. With a little creativity and planning, you can enjoy a variety of delicious and nutritious snacks that support your overall health and well-being. Whether you prefer fresh fruits and vegetables, protein-packed options, or whole grains, there are endless possibilities to explore. By choosing wholesome ingredients and being mindful of portion sizes, you can make snacking a positive and enjoyable part of your daily routine. Incorporating healthy snacks into your daily routine also provides an opportunity to set a positive example for others, particularly children. By demonstrating that nutritious foods can be enjoyable and satisfying, you can help instill lifelong healthy eating habits in young ones. Involving children in the preparation of snacks, such as assembling their own fruit kebabs or helping to mix ingredients for homemade granola bars, can make them more enthusiastic about eating healthy.

Party Platters and Boards

Creating a stunning party platter or board is an art form that combines culinary skills, creativity, and an understanding of flavors and textures. These versatile spreads are perfect for any gathering, offering a variety of foods that cater to different tastes and dietary preferences. Crafting the perfect party platter involves thoughtful selection of ingredients, attention to presentation, and a touch of personal flair.

Start with the foundation of any good platter: the board itself. Wooden boards, marble slabs, or large ceramic plates all make excellent bases. The choice of board sets the tone for your platter, so consider the aesthetic you want to achieve. A rustic wooden board gives a casual, homey feel, while a sleek marble slab can elevate the presentation to a more sophisticated level.

Next, think about the different components you want to include. A well-rounded party platter typically features a balance of proteins, cheeses, fruits, vegetables, nuts, and condiments. The key is to offer a variety of flavors and textures to keep things interesting. For proteins, consider cured meats like prosciutto, salami, or chorizo. These meats not only add a savory element but also pair well with a range of cheeses and condiments.

Cheeses are a star attraction on any platter. Aim for a mix of hard, soft, and blue cheeses to provide a variety of tastes and textures. Hard cheeses like aged cheddar or gouda offer a firm bite and rich flavor, while soft cheeses such as brie or camembert bring a creamy, decadent touch. Blue cheeses like gorgonzola or Roquefort add a bold, tangy note. Arrange the cheeses in different sections of the board, cutting some into bite-sized pieces and leaving others whole for guests to slice themselves.

Fruits and vegetables add color, freshness, and a natural sweetness to the platter. Choose fruits that are in season for the best flavor and juiciness. Grapes, figs, and berries are classic choices that pair wonderfully with cheese and meat. For a pop of color and a refreshing crunch, include sliced vegetables like bell peppers, cucumbers, and cherry tomatoes. These also serve as great dippers for any spreads or dips you decide to include.

Nuts and seeds provide a satisfying crunch and are a great way to fill in gaps on the board. Almonds, walnuts, and pistachios are popular choices. They can be roasted and salted or left plain, depending on your preference. Not only do they add texture, but they also bring healthy fats and protein to the mix.

Condiments and spreads are essential for adding flavor and variety. Think about including a mix of sweet and savory options. Honey or fruit preserves pair beautifully with cheese, while mustards and tapenades complement meats. A good hummus or a creamy spinach dip can be a hit with both vegetables and crackers. Place these in small bowls or ramekins to keep them contained and prevent them from spreading onto other items.

Bread and crackers are the vehicles for enjoying all the delicious components of your platter. Offer a variety of options to cater to different tastes. Sliced baguette, breadsticks, and an assortment of crackers provide plenty of choices. Make sure to include gluten-free options if any of your guests have dietary restrictions.

Presentation is crucial when it comes to party platters. Start by placing the larger items first, such as bowls of dip, whole cheeses, and clusters of grapes. Then, arrange the smaller items around them, filling in gaps and creating a visually appealing display. Vary the shapes and sizes of the items to add interest. For example, roll or fold slices of meat, fan out slices of cheese, and pile nuts in small mounds. Use fresh herbs like rosemary or thyme to add a touch of green and a fragrant element.

Consider the flow of the platter. You want it to be easy for guests to navigate and access all the different components. Group similar items together, but also mix things up to encourage people to try new combinations. For example, place a small bowl of honey next to a blue cheese and some apple slices to suggest a delicious pairing.

Think about the overall color palette of your board. A mix of vibrant and muted colors creates a visually appealing contrast. The deep reds of cured meats, the golden hues of cheeses, the bright greens of vegetables, and the rich purples of grapes all contribute to a beautiful and appetizing display.

Don't forget about the importance of replenishing the platter throughout the event. As guests enjoy the food, certain items may run out faster than others. Have extra supplies on hand to refill as needed, keeping the platter looking abundant and inviting.

For a more personalized touch, consider incorporating themed elements into your platter. If you're hosting a holiday party, use seasonal ingredients and decorations. For example, during the winter holidays, add some sprigs of pine or cranberries for a festive look. For a summer gathering, include tropical fruits like mango and pineapple, and decorate with edible flowers.

Finally, remember that the goal of a party platter is to bring people together over good food. Encourage guests to explore different flavors and combinations, and enjoy the process of creating and sharing a beautiful spread. With thoughtful selection and presentation, your party platter will not only be a feast for the eyes but also a memorable highlight of your event.

Crafting a party platter or board is more than just assembling food; it's about creating an experience. Each bite should offer a delightful mix of flavors and textures, inviting guests to savor and enjoy. By paying attention to the details and infusing your own creativity, you can create a platter that is as enjoyable to look at as it is to eat. Whether for a small gathering or a large celebration, a well-made party platter is sure to impress and delight your guests, making your event truly special. To elevate your party platter even further, consider incorporating some unique and artisanal elements. Specialty items like truffle-infused cheese, artisanal charcuterie, or gourmet crackers can add a touch of luxury and uniqueness to your spread. These high-quality ingredients offer exceptional flavors and textures that can turn an ordinary platter into an extraordinary one.

Chapter 4

Soups and Salads

Hearty and Comforting Soups

There's something inherently soothing about a bowl of hearty, comforting soup. It has the power to warm you from the inside out, providing not just sustenance but also a sense of well-being. Whether it's a chilly winter evening or a rainy spring day, soups can offer a perfect blend of warmth, flavor, and nutrition. Crafting the perfect soup involves understanding the balance of ingredients, mastering cooking techniques, and adding a personal touch to create a dish that's both delicious and comforting.

Start with a solid foundation: the broth. A rich, well-made broth is the backbone of any good soup. While store-bought broths can be convenient, making your own can significantly enhance the flavor. Begin with a basic stock, whether it's chicken, beef, vegetable, or even seafood. Simmer bones or vegetables with aromatics like onions, garlic, carrots, and celery for several hours to extract maximum flavor. Season the broth with salt, pepper, and herbs such as bay leaves, thyme, or rosemary. Strain the stock to remove solids, and you're left with a liquid gold that serves as the perfect base for your soup.

Next, consider the primary ingredients that will define your soup. Vegetables, proteins, grains, and legumes are all excellent choices, each bringing their own unique textures and flavors. For a vegetable-based soup, use a variety of fresh, seasonal produce. Root vegetables like carrots, potatoes, and parsnips add sweetness and body, while leafy greens like kale or spinach provide color and nutrients. For a protein-rich soup, include ingredients such as chicken, beef, or beans. Chicken noodle soup is a classic example where tender chunks of chicken and al dente pasta create a satisfying, hearty dish.

The method of cooking can greatly influence the final result. Sautéing your vegetables before adding them to the broth can deepen their flavors through caramelization. This step, known as sweating, involves cooking the vegetables over medium heat with a bit of oil until they soften and release their juices. For a richer taste, deglaze the pot with a splash of wine or vinegar to lift the fond, the brown bits stuck to the bottom, into the soup.

Incorporating grains and legumes can add both substance and nutrition to your soup. Barley, rice, and quinoa are excellent choices that can transform a light broth into a filling meal. Legumes like lentils, chickpeas, and split peas not only add protein but also a creamy texture when cooked down. For example, a classic lentil soup combines earthy lentils with aromatic vegetables and spices, resulting in a comforting and nutritious dish.

Herbs and spices play a crucial role in defining the flavor profile of your soup. Fresh herbs like parsley, cilantro, and dill can brighten up a soup, adding a fresh, green note. Dried herbs and spices such as cumin, coriander, and paprika can provide depth and warmth. Don't be afraid to experiment with spice blends from different cuisines to create unique and exciting flavors. For instance, adding curry powder to a butternut squash soup can give it an exotic twist, while a touch of smoked paprika can add a layer of complexity to a simple tomato soup.

Cream and dairy can add richness and a velvety texture to your soup. A classic example is a creamy potato leek soup, where the addition of cream transforms the dish into a luxurious treat. If you prefer a dairy-free option, coconut milk can be an excellent substitute, offering a creamy texture and a subtle sweetness. Pureeing part or all of the soup can also create a smooth, thick consistency. Use an immersion blender for convenience, or carefully transfer the soup to a regular blender in batches.

Garnishes are the final touch that can elevate your soup from good to great. Freshly chopped herbs, a drizzle of olive oil, a sprinkle of cheese, or a dollop of yogurt can add color, texture, and additional flavors. Croutons or a slice of crusty bread can provide a satisfying crunch and make the meal more complete. For a touch of luxury, consider adding a swirl of truffle oil or a few shavings of Parmesan cheese.

Presentation matters, even with something as humble as soup. Serve your soup in warmed bowls to keep it hot longer. A rustic, earthenware bowl can enhance the homey feel, while a sleek, modern bowl can make the dish feel more sophisticated. Pair the soup with a simple side salad or a piece of artisan bread to round out the meal.

Soups are also incredibly versatile and forgiving, making them perfect for experimentation. Don't be afraid to improvise based on what you have on hand. Leftover roast chicken can become the star of a chicken and vegetable soup, while a surplus of tomatoes can be transformed into a rich, flavorful tomato basil soup. The key is to balance flavors, textures, and ingredients to create a harmonious dish.

One of the greatest benefits of homemade soup is its ability to be prepared in advance and stored for later. Most soups taste even better the next day as the flavors meld and develop. Make a large batch and freeze portions for quick, healthy meals during busy weeks. Reheat gently on the stove to preserve the texture and flavor.

In summary, creating hearty and comforting soups involves a blend of quality ingredients, thoughtful preparation, and a bit of creativity. By mastering the basics and experimenting with different flavors and techniques, you can craft soups that are not only delicious and nutritious but also deeply satisfying. Whether you're making a classic chicken noodle soup, a spicy lentil stew, or a creamy vegetable bisque, the process of making soup is as rewarding as the final product. It's a culinary journey that brings warmth, comfort, and a sense of home to anyone who takes a spoonful. The versatility of soups makes them an ideal dish for accommodating various dietary restrictions and preferences. For those who follow a vegetarian or vegan diet, hearty vegetable soups can be a great option. Consider a minestrone packed with beans, pasta, and a variety of vegetables, or a spicy black bean soup with a hint of smoky chipotle. Both are rich in flavor and nutrients, providing a balanced meal without the need for meat or animal products.

Light and Refreshing Salads

Light and refreshing salads are a delightful way to enhance any meal. They are versatile, nutritious, and can be tailored to fit any dietary preference or seasonal availability. Creating a perfect salad involves understanding the balance of flavors, textures, and colors while also considering the nutritional benefits. This chapter delves into the essentials of crafting salads that are not only light and refreshing but also satisfying and delicious.

The foundation of any good salad starts with fresh, high-quality ingredients. Leafy greens are often the base, providing a crisp and crunchy texture. Varieties such as romaine, arugula, spinach, and kale each bring unique flavors and nutritional profiles. Arugula, for instance, offers a peppery bite, while spinach has a mild, slightly sweet taste. Mixing different greens can create a more complex flavor and texture.

Vegetables add color, crunch, and a wide array of nutrients. Think beyond the usual tomatoes and cucumbers. Bell peppers, radishes, carrots, and beets can add vibrant hues and various textures. Thinly sliced fennel or shaved Brussels sprouts can introduce unexpected flavors and a delightful crunch. Don't shy away from incorporating fruits; strawberries, oranges, apples, and pears can provide a sweet contrast to the savory elements.

The protein component is crucial for making a salad more substantial. Grilled chicken, shrimp, or tofu are excellent choices for a light and refreshing salad. For a plant-based option, consider adding beans, lentils, or quinoa. Cheese, such as feta, goat cheese, or mozzarella, can also offer a creamy texture and rich flavor. Nuts and seeds like almonds, sunflower seeds, or pumpkin seeds add crunch and a dose of healthy fats.

Dressings are the final touch that can elevate a salad from good to great. A simple vinaigrette made with olive oil, vinegar or lemon juice, and a touch of mustard is a classic choice. Experiment with different oils, such as walnut or avocado oil, and various vinegars like balsamic, apple cider, or red wine vinegar. Add herbs, garlic, or shallots to the dressing for extra depth of flavor. Yogurt-based dressings can also provide a creamy alternative without the heaviness of mayonnaise.

Balancing flavors is an art. A successful salad often includes elements of sweetness, acidity, bitterness, and saltiness. For example, a salad with bitter arugula can be balanced with sweet cherry tomatoes and tangy lemon vinaigrette. Salty feta cheese can complement the sweetness of watermelon slices. The key is to taste as you go and adjust the seasoning and ingredients accordingly.

Textures play a significant role in creating an enjoyable salad. Combining crisp, crunchy vegetables with creamy, soft elements makes each bite interesting. Think about adding roasted vegetables for a slightly chewy texture or fresh herbs for a burst of flavor. A handful of crispy croutons or a sprinkle of seeds can add the perfect finishing touch.

Salads can be seasonal, highlighting the freshest produce available. In spring, tender greens, radishes, and peas can create a vibrant mix. Summer is the perfect time for juicy tomatoes, cucumbers, and fresh herbs. Fall brings heartier options like roasted squash, apples, and nuts, while winter salads can feature citrus fruits, hearty greens, and root vegetables. Seasonal ingredients ensure that the salad is not only delicious but also at its nutritional peak.

Presentation is another aspect that can make a salad more appealing. Use a variety of colors and shapes to make the salad visually interesting. Slicing vegetables in different ways—thinly, julienned, or in rounds—can create a more dynamic look. Arranging the ingredients thoughtfully on a plate or in a bowl can make the salad look as good as it tastes.

To illustrate, let's walk through creating a light and refreshing summer salad. Start with a mix of baby spinach and arugula as the base. Add thinly sliced cucumbers, halved cherry tomatoes, and diced yellow bell pepper for color and crunch. Toss in some fresh strawberries for sweetness and a handful of crumbled feta cheese. For the protein, add some grilled shrimp seasoned with a bit of lemon and garlic. Finish with a simple lemon vinaigrette made with olive oil, lemon juice, Dijon mustard, and a touch of honey. Garnish with a sprinkle of sunflower seeds for extra crunch. This salad is a perfect example of balancing flavors, textures, and colors to create a dish that is both light and satisfying.

Exploring international flavors can also bring new life to your salads. A Greek salad with tomatoes, cucumbers, red onions, Kalamata olives, and feta cheese dressed with olive oil and oregano is a classic. A Thai-inspired salad might include shredded carrots, bell peppers, and cabbage, with a dressing made from lime juice, fish sauce, and a touch of sugar, topped with fresh cilantro and peanuts. These variations can add excitement and variety to your salad repertoire.

For those who enjoy a bit of sweetness, fruit-based salads can be a delightful change. A watermelon and feta salad with mint leaves and a drizzle of balsamic reduction is a refreshing option. Another idea is a mixed berry salad with blueberries, strawberries, and raspberries, tossed with baby spinach and a light poppy seed dressing. These salads are perfect for hot summer days when you crave something light and cooling.

Incorporating grains can make salads more filling without losing their lightness. Quinoa, farro, or bulgur can add a nutty flavor and chewy texture. A salad with cooked quinoa, chopped cucumbers, cherry tomatoes, red onion, and parsley, dressed with lemon juice and olive oil, is both refreshing and substantial. These grains also provide additional protein and fiber, making the salad a complete meal.

Don't forget about herbs and spices. Fresh herbs like basil, mint, cilantro, and dill can add a burst of flavor. Spices such as cumin, coriander, and smoked paprika can be sprinkled on proteins or mixed into dressings to enhance the overall taste. These small additions can make a big difference in the final dish.

Finally, it's important to remember that salads should be enjoyable and reflect your personal taste. Don't be afraid to experiment with different combinations of ingredients and dressings until you find your perfect mix. The goal is to create a salad that is not only light and refreshing but also something you look forward to eating.

In conclusion, light and refreshing salads are a versatile and nutritious addition to any meal. By focusing on fresh ingredients, balancing flavors and textures, and incorporating seasonal produce, you can create salads that are both delicious and satisfying. Whether you prefer a simple green salad or a more complex combination of vegetables, proteins, and fruits, the possibilities are endless. So next time you're looking for a light and refreshing meal, consider building a salad that delights the senses and nourishes the body. Another important aspect of crafting light and refreshing salads is understanding the role of temperature and preparation techniques. Cold salads can be incredibly refreshing, especially during hot weather. However, incorporating warm elements can add a new dimension of flavor and texture.

Dressings and Vinaigrettes

Dressings and vinaigrettes are the soul of any salad, transforming simple greens and vegetables into a harmonious blend of flavors. They add the necessary moisture, enhance textures, and bring together the various elements in a salad, elevating it from a mere mix of ingredients to a cohesive dish. Mastering a few essential dressings and vinaigrettes can open up a world of culinary possibilities, allowing you to experiment and create your own signature blends.

At their core, vinaigrettes are a simple emulsion of oil and vinegar, often enhanced with various seasonings.

A classic vinaigrette typically follows a basic ratio of three parts oil to one part vinegar. This balance can be adjusted based on personal taste and the specific ingredients in the salad. For instance, a salad with robust, bitter greens like arugula might benefit from a slightly higher vinegar ratio to cut through the bitterness, while a salad featuring sweeter elements like fruit might be best complemented by a milder vinaigrette.

The choice of oil and vinegar is fundamental to the flavor profile of the vinaigrette. Extra virgin olive oil is a popular choice for its rich, fruity flavor, but other oils such as walnut, avocado, and sesame oil can bring their unique characteristics to the mix. Each oil has its own smoke point and flavor profile, which can influence the overall taste and texture of the dressing. For example, walnut oil adds a nutty depth perfect for fall salads with roasted squash and apples, while sesame oil imparts an unmistakable Asian flair ideal for salads with ingredients like cabbage and carrots.

Vinegars also come in a variety of forms, each providing a distinct acidity and flavor. Balsamic vinegar, with its sweet and tangy notes, pairs wonderfully with salads featuring fruits and rich cheeses. Apple cider vinegar offers a milder, fruity tang that works well with most greens and vegetables. Red wine vinegar is a versatile choice, adding a sharp, robust acidity that can enhance a wide range of salad components. Less common but equally delightful options include rice vinegar, which is light and slightly sweet, perfect for Asian-inspired salads, and sherry vinegar, which brings a complex, nutty flavor that can elevate simple greens.

Beyond the basic oil and vinegar, the addition of mustard, honey, garlic, and herbs can transform a simple vinaigrette into something extraordinary. Mustard, particularly Dijon, acts as an emulsifier, helping to blend the oil and vinegar into a smooth, cohesive dressing while adding a subtle, spicy kick. Honey or maple syrup can balance the acidity of the vinegar with a touch of sweetness, creating a more rounded flavor. Fresh garlic, either minced or crushed, infuses the vinaigrette with a pungent, savory depth that can enhance the overall complexity of the salad. Herbs such as basil, thyme, and dill add freshness and can be tailored to complement the specific ingredients in the salad.

Creamy dressings, while richer than vinaigrettes, offer their own set of possibilities. These dressings often use a base of yogurt, mayonnaise, or buttermilk to create a smooth, luxurious texture. Greek yogurt is an excellent choice for a lighter, tangy dressing that still provides creaminess without the heaviness of mayonnaise. Buttermilk, with its slightly sour taste, can add a tangy richness that works well in dressings like ranch or blue cheese. For a vegan alternative, consider using avocado or tahini to create a creamy texture that is both satisfying and nutritious.

The flavorings for creamy dressings are as varied as those for vinaigrettes. Fresh herbs like chives, parsley, and cilantro can add a burst of freshness, while spices such as cumin, smoked paprika, and curry powder can introduce a warm, complex undertone. Acidic components like lemon juice or apple cider vinegar are crucial to balance the richness of the creamy base, ensuring the dressing is not overwhelmingly heavy.

Balancing the flavors in any dressing or vinaigrette is crucial. Taste as you go and adjust the seasoning to achieve the desired balance of acidity, sweetness, and saltiness. A pinch of salt can enhance the overall flavor, while a dash of pepper can add a subtle heat. Some dressings might benefit from the addition of finely grated cheese, such as Parmesan, which adds umami and depth.

Storage and preparation of dressings are also important considerations. Homemade dressings and vinaigrettes typically have a shorter shelf life than store-bought varieties since they lack preservatives. Store them in a sealed container in the refrigerator, and use within a week for optimal freshness. When preparing a dressing, whisking by hand is often sufficient, but using a blender or food processor can create a smoother, more emulsified consistency. If the dressing separates during storage, simply give it a good shake or whisk before using.

Experimenting with different ingredients and techniques can lead to the discovery of new favorite dressings. For instance, blending roasted red peppers into a vinaigrette can add a sweet, smoky flavor that pairs beautifully with Mediterranean salads. Adding a spoonful of miso paste to a creamy dressing can introduce a savory, umami element that enhances a variety of salads. The possibilities are endless, and the process of experimentation can be both fun and rewarding.

Dressings and vinaigrettes are not limited to salads alone. They can be used as marinades for proteins, as dips for vegetables, or even drizzled over roasted vegetables to add an extra layer of flavor. A versatile vinaigrette can double as a marinade for chicken, infusing it with flavor before grilling. A creamy dressing can serve as a dip for raw vegetables or a spread for sandwiches and wraps.

Understanding the fundamentals of creating dressings and vinaigrettes can greatly enhance your culinary repertoire. By mastering a few basic recipes and techniques, you can easily adapt and create your own variations to suit any salad or dish. The key is to balance the flavors, experiment with different ingredients, and most importantly, have fun in the process. Dressings and vinaigrettes are the finishing touch that can elevate your salads from ordinary to extraordinary, making them a staple in any kitchen. One of the most gratifying aspects of crafting your own dressings and vinaigrettes is the ability to tailor them to your specific dietary needs and preferences. For those looking to reduce their calorie intake, vinaigrettes made with lighter oils or a higher vinegar ratio can be a great option. Conversely, for individuals seeking more richness, incorporating ingredients like tahini, nut butters, or even a touch of cream can add a luxurious texture without the need for traditional heavy bases.

Seasonal Soup Specials

Seasonal soup specials have the power to warm hearts and nourish souls, offering a delightful way to savor the flavors of each season. They provide an opportunity to use fresh, seasonal ingredients that are at their peak, ensuring the most vibrant flavors and nutrients. Crafting soups that align with the seasons not only celebrates the bounty of nature but also brings variety to our dining tables, making each bowl a unique experience.

Spring is a time of renewal, and the soups that emerge from this season reflect that spirit. As the earth awakens from its winter slumber, tender greens and early vegetables begin to appear. A classic spring soup is the vibrant and refreshing pea soup. Fresh peas, with their natural sweetness, form the base of this bright green soup. Adding fresh mint leaves enhances the flavor, creating a perfect harmony of sweet and herbaceous notes. A touch of cream or a dollop of crème fraîche can add richness, though a lighter, broth-based version is equally delightful. Another spring favorite is asparagus soup. Asparagus, when cooked until tender and blended, yields a velvety texture and a delicate flavor. Lemon zest or a squeeze of lemon juice can brighten the taste, making it an invigorating start to a meal.

As the days grow warmer, summer brings a bounty of produce, and the soups of this season take advantage of the abundance. Gazpacho, a chilled Spanish soup, is a quintessential summer dish. Made from ripe tomatoes, cucumbers, bell peppers, onions, and garlic, it's a refreshing blend that's both hydrating and satisfying. The vegetables are typically pureed together with olive oil and vinegar, resulting in a vibrant, tangy soup that's served cold, making it perfect for hot days. Another summer delight is corn chowder. Fresh corn, when in season, is incredibly sweet and juicy. A simple chowder made with corn, potatoes, and a touch of cream can be both hearty and light, capturing the essence of summer in every spoonful. Adding fresh herbs like basil or cilantro can introduce a burst of freshness that complements the sweetness of the corn.

Autumn, with its crisp air and falling leaves, calls for heartier, warming soups. This is the season of root vegetables and squashes, and their robust flavors lend themselves beautifully to comforting soups. Butternut squash soup is a staple of the fall. The natural sweetness of roasted butternut squash, when pureed with onions, garlic, and a hint of nutmeg or cinnamon, creates a rich, creamy soup that's both soothing and satisfying. For an added depth of flavor, some recipes incorporate apples or pears, which pair wonderfully with the squash. Another autumn favorite is mushroom soup. Earthy mushrooms, sautéed with shallots and garlic, create a deeply flavored base. Adding a splash of sherry or white wine can enhance the complexity of the soup, while a swirl of cream or a sprinkle of fresh thyme can add a touch of elegance.

Winter is the season for robust, hearty soups that can warm you from the inside out. This is the time for root vegetables, legumes, and sturdy greens, all of which can withstand long cooking times and develop deep, rich flavors. A classic winter soup is beef and barley soup. Tender chunks of beef, simmered with barley, carrots, celery, and onions, create a nourishing and filling soup that's perfect for cold winter days. The barley adds a pleasant chewiness, while the beef broth, often enhanced with a splash of red wine, provides a rich, savory base. Lentil soup is another winter staple. Lentils, with their earthy flavor and hearty texture, combine beautifully with root vegetables and greens like spinach or kale. A touch of cumin or smoked paprika can add warmth and depth to the soup, making it both comforting and nutritious.

Crafting seasonal soups also allows for creativity and experimentation. Incorporating unexpected ingredients or new flavor combinations can lead to delightful discoveries. For instance, adding a touch of coconut milk to a traditional pumpkin soup can introduce a creamy, exotic twist. Similarly, blending roasted red peppers into a tomato soup can add a smoky sweetness that elevates the overall flavor profile.

The preparation and presentation of seasonal soups can also enhance the dining experience. Using homemade broths and stocks can significantly improve the flavor and nutritional value of the soup. A rich chicken or vegetable stock, simmered with herbs and aromatics, can provide a robust base that elevates even the simplest of soups. For a more refined presentation, consider garnishing your soups with fresh herbs, a drizzle of high-quality olive oil, or a sprinkle of toasted seeds or nuts. These finishing touches not only add flavor and texture but also make the soup visually appealing.

Seasonal soups are also a wonderful way to incorporate more vegetables and whole foods into your diet. They allow you to take full advantage of the nutritional benefits of seasonal produce, which is often fresher and more flavorful than out-of-season alternatives. By focusing on what's in season, you can also support local farmers and reduce the environmental impact associated with transporting out-of-season produce.

In addition to their culinary and nutritional benefits, seasonal soups offer a sense of connection to the natural rhythms of the year. They encourage us to slow down and savor the unique flavors and textures that each season brings. Whether it's the first taste of a light, herb-infused spring soup, the refreshing chill of a summer gazpacho, the comforting warmth of an autumn squash soup, or the hearty nourishment of a winter barley soup, each bowl tells a story of the season and the ingredients that define it.

In closing, embracing the concept of seasonal soup specials can transform your approach to cooking and eating. It encourages mindfulness and creativity, allowing you to celebrate the diversity of each season's produce. By mastering a few basic techniques and experimenting with different ingredients and flavor combinations, you can create a repertoire of soups that not only nourish the body but also delight the senses. Seasonal soups are a testament to the beauty and bounty of nature, offering a simple yet profound way to connect with the changing seasons and the world around us. As you continue to explore the world of seasonal soup specials, consider how these soups can be integrated into your meal plans to create balanced and fulfilling diets throughout the year. Each season's offerings can be adapted to fit various dietary needs and preferences, ensuring that everyone at the table can enjoy the benefits of these delicious, nutrient-rich dishes.

Salads for Every Occasion

Salads for every occasion offer a versatile and vibrant way to celebrate the bounty of fresh ingredients, providing both nourishment and delight. Whether it's a light starter, a hearty main course, or a festive dish for special gatherings, salads can be customized to fit any meal or event. Their adaptability makes them an essential component of any culinary repertoire, allowing for endless creativity and variation.

An everyday salad can be as simple or as complex as you like. A basic green salad, composed of fresh lettuce, arugula, or spinach, can be quickly elevated with the addition of a few key ingredients. Consider adding sliced cucumbers, cherry tomatoes, and red onion for a burst of color and crunch. A handful of toasted nuts or seeds can introduce a delightful texture, while crumbled cheese, such as feta or goat cheese, adds a creamy, tangy element. The dressing, whether a classic vinaigrette or a creamy ranch, ties everything together, enhancing the flavors without overwhelming them.

For a more substantial salad, consider incorporating proteins such as grilled chicken, shrimp, or tofu. A grilled chicken Caesar salad, for instance, combines the smoky flavor of the chicken with the crispness of Romaine lettuce and the bold taste of Parmesan cheese. The Caesar dressing, rich and garlicky, coats each bite, making it a satisfying and balanced meal. Similarly, a shrimp and avocado salad offers a delightful combination of textures and flavors. The creamy avocado contrasts with the firm, slightly sweet shrimp, while a citrusy dressing adds a refreshing finish.

Salads can also serve as a canvas for showcasing seasonal produce. In the spring, a salad of fresh asparagus, peas, and radishes celebrates the tender new growth of the season. Tossed with a light lemon vinaigrette and topped with fresh herbs, this salad is both vibrant and refreshing. Summer brings an abundance of tomatoes, cucumbers, and bell peppers, perfect for a Mediterranean-inspired salad. Adding olives, feta cheese, and a drizzle of olive oil transforms these simple ingredients into a dish bursting with flavor.

Autumn offers heartier ingredients like roasted squash, apples, and nuts. A roasted butternut squash and kale salad, for example, combines the sweet, caramelized flavor of the squash with the robust texture of kale. Adding dried cranberries and pecans introduces a sweet and nutty element, while a maple Dijon dressing ties all the flavors together. In winter, root vegetables like beets and carrots can be roasted and added to salads for a warm, comforting twist. A beet and goat cheese salad, with its striking colors and earthy flavors, can be a beautiful and delicious addition to any winter meal.

Special occasions call for salads that are not only delicious but also visually impressive. For a festive holiday gathering, consider a pomegranate and pear salad. The jewel-like pomegranate seeds add a burst of color and tartness, while the sweet, juicy pear slices provide a lovely contrast. Tossed with mixed greens, blue cheese, and candied pecans, and dressed with a balsamic reduction, this salad is both elegant and flavorful.

For a summer picnic or barbecue, a classic potato salad is always a crowd-pleaser. Boiled potatoes, mixed with hard-boiled eggs, celery, and onions, and dressed with a creamy mayonnaise-based dressing, create a comforting and satisfying dish. Adding a touch of mustard and fresh herbs can elevate the flavor, making it a standout side dish.

When planning salads for every occasion, it's important to consider the balance of flavors and textures. A successful salad often includes a mix of sweet, salty, sour, and bitter elements, as well as a variety of textures from crunchy to creamy. This balance can be achieved by thoughtfully combining ingredients and experimenting with different dressings and seasonings.

The dressing is a crucial component of any salad, as it can enhance or overpower the other ingredients. A simple vinaigrette, made with olive oil, vinegar, mustard, and a touch of honey, is a versatile option that can be adapted with different herbs and seasonings. Creamy dressings, such as ranch or blue cheese, are best suited for heartier salads with bold flavors. When making a dressing, it's important to taste and adjust the seasoning as needed, ensuring that it complements the salad without overwhelming it.

Presentation is also key when serving salads for special occasions. Using a variety of colors and arranging the ingredients thoughtfully can make the salad visually appealing. For a more polished presentation, consider layering the ingredients rather than tossing them together. This not only looks beautiful but also allows guests to appreciate the individual components of the salad.

In addition to their culinary appeal, salads offer numerous health benefits. They are an excellent way to incorporate a variety of vegetables and fruits into your diet, providing essential vitamins, minerals, and fiber. Including a source of protein, such as chicken, fish, beans, or nuts, can make the salad a complete and balanced meal. For those following specific dietary plans, salads can be easily adapted to fit low-carb, gluten-free, or vegan requirements.

Incorporating grains into salads can add both substance and nutritional value. Quinoa, farro, and barley are excellent options that provide a hearty base for a variety of ingredients. A quinoa salad with black beans, corn, and avocado, dressed with a lime-cilantro vinaigrette, offers a flavorful and protein-packed meal. Farro, with its chewy texture and nutty flavor, pairs well with roasted vegetables and a tangy balsamic dressing.

Exploring global flavors can also inspire new and exciting salad combinations. A Thai-inspired salad, featuring shredded cabbage, carrots, and bell peppers, tossed with a peanut dressing and topped with fresh cilantro and chopped peanuts, offers a vibrant and flavorful experience. A Middle Eastern tabbouleh, made with bulgur wheat, parsley, tomatoes, and mint, dressed with lemon juice and olive oil, is a refreshing and herbaceous option.

Salads can also play a role in reducing food waste by utilizing leftovers and seasonal produce. Leftover roasted vegetables, grains, or proteins can be repurposed into a delicious salad the next day. This not only saves time and resources but also encourages creativity in the kitchen.

For those who enjoy gardening, growing your own salad ingredients can be a rewarding experience. Fresh herbs, lettuce, tomatoes, and cucumbers can be easily grown in a garden or even in containers on a balcony. Harvesting your own produce ensures the freshest ingredients and can make the process of creating salads even more enjoyable.

In conclusion, salads for every occasion are a testament to the versatility and beauty of fresh ingredients. They offer endless possibilities for creativity, allowing you to explore different flavors, textures, and cultural inspirations. By focusing on balance, presentation, and the use of high-quality ingredients, you can create salads that are not only delicious but also nourishing and visually stunning. Whether it's a simple everyday salad or an impressive dish for a special gathering, salads have the power to delight and satisfy, making them an essential part of any culinary repertoire. Experimenting with different types of greens can add variety and interest to your salads. While traditional lettuce and spinach are always reliable choices, consider branching out to more unique options like arugula, watercress, or mizuna. Arugula adds a peppery kick that pairs well with sweet fruits and tangy cheeses, while watercress offers a slightly bitter, peppery flavor that complements rich, creamy dressings. Mizuna, with its feathery leaves and mild mustard flavor, can add an unexpected twist to your salad repertoire.

96

Chapter 5

Weeknight Dinners

One-Pot Wonders

A one-pot meal can be the savior of a busy weeknight, the star of a cozy weekend gathering, or the go-to for anyone seeking a delicious and satisfying dish without the daunting prospect of a mountain of dirty dishes. The beauty of one-pot wonders lies in their simplicity and the magic that happens when ingredients are allowed to mingle and meld in a single vessel. These dishes harmonize flavors, make the most of your ingredients, and often improve with time, making them perfect for leftovers.

One-pot wonders encompass a vast array of culinary traditions and techniques, from hearty stews and soups to elegant risottos and fragrant curries. The key to mastering these dishes is understanding the fundamental principles that make them work: layering flavors, managing cooking times, and balancing textures.

Imagine a classic French beef bourguignon. This dish starts with browning chunks of beef in a heavy-bottomed pot to develop a deep, caramelized flavor. After removing the meat, you use the same pot to sauté onions, carrots, and garlic, scraping up the browned bits from the bottom – these bits are packed with flavor. Adding tomato paste and cooking it briefly enhances the dish's depth. Then, you return the beef to the pot, along with red wine, beef broth, and herbs. The whole mix simmers slowly, allowing the meat to become tender and the flavors to meld beautifully. The resulting dish is a rich, hearty stew that tastes like it took days to prepare, yet it all came together in one pot.

The versatility of one-pot meals is truly astounding. Take, for instance, a simple chicken and rice dish. By sautéing some onions, garlic, and bell peppers in a large skillet, then adding seasoned chicken thighs and allowing them to brown, you're building a robust flavor base. Next, you add rice and chicken broth, cover the skillet, and let it simmer until the rice is tender and the chicken is cooked through. The rice absorbs the flavors of the chicken and vegetables, creating a cohesive and comforting meal. You can easily adapt this basic formula with different herbs, spices, and additional ingredients like beans or vegetables to create endless variations.

For those who enjoy Asian cuisine, the concept of one-pot meals is exemplified in dishes like Japanese hot pots or Chinese clay pot rice. A Japanese hot pot, or nabe, involves simmering a variety of ingredients like thinly sliced meats, tofu, vegetables, and noodles in a flavorful broth. The communal aspect of cooking and eating directly from the pot adds to the experience, making it both a social and culinary delight. Similarly, Chinese clay pot rice involves cooking rice, meats, and vegetables together in a clay pot, allowing the rice to develop a crispy bottom layer, which is considered a delicacy.

One-pot pasta dishes have gained popularity for their convenience and the way they allow pasta to absorb the flavors of the sauce as it cooks. A classic example is pasta puttanesca. In a large pot, sauté garlic, anchovies, and red pepper flakes in olive oil. Add diced tomatoes, olives, capers, and a splash of white wine, then stir in the uncooked pasta and water or broth. As the pasta cooks, it absorbs the tangy, savory flavors of the sauce, resulting in a dish that's both deeply flavorful and incredibly easy to make.

The charm of one-pot meals also extends to breakfast and brunch. Consider a hearty shakshuka, a North African and Middle Eastern dish of eggs poached in a spicy tomato and pepper sauce. You start by sautéing onions, bell peppers, and garlic in olive oil, then add tomatoes and spices like cumin, paprika, and cayenne. Once the sauce has thickened, you make wells in the sauce and crack eggs into them, allowing them to cook gently. The result is a vibrant, flavorful dish that's perfect for dipping bread into and sharing with friends and family.

When preparing one-pot meals, choosing the right pot is crucial. A Dutch oven, for example, is ideal for slow-cooked stews, braises, and soups due to its excellent heat retention and even cooking. A large, deep skillet works well for pasta dishes and rice-based meals, while a wok is perfect for stir-fries and Asian-inspired dishes. The right pot not only ensures even cooking but also enhances the flavors by allowing proper caramelization and deglazing.

Balancing flavors in a one-pot meal often involves a careful dance of seasoning at each stage of cooking. Starting with a flavorful base, such as sautéed onions, garlic, and spices, sets the tone for the dish. Deglazing the pot with wine, broth, or other liquids captures all the browned bits stuck to the bottom, infusing the dish with a rich depth of flavor. Adding herbs and spices throughout the cooking process, rather than all at once, allows their flavors to develop and meld harmoniously. Finally, a splash of acid, such as lemon juice or vinegar, added at the end can brighten and balance the dish, cutting through the richness and enhancing the overall taste.

One-pot meals also offer the opportunity to incorporate a variety of textures. Adding ingredients in stages ensures that everything is cooked to perfection. For instance, in a vegetable stew, root vegetables like potatoes and carrots can be added early to allow them time to soften, while more delicate vegetables like peas or spinach can be added towards the end to retain their texture and vibrant color. Similarly, adding a handful of nuts or seeds just before serving can introduce a delightful crunch.

Cooking one-pot meals can also be an exercise in creativity and resourcefulness. Leftovers and pantry staples can often be transformed into a satisfying dish with the addition of fresh ingredients and thoughtful seasoning. A simple vegetable and bean chili, for example, can be made with canned tomatoes, beans, and whatever vegetables you have on hand. By sautéing onions and spices first, then adding tomatoes, beans, and vegetables, you create a hearty, nutritious meal that's perfect for batch cooking and serving throughout the week.

Incorporating grains into one-pot meals is another way to create satisfying, balanced dishes. A classic example is a pilaf, where rice or other grains are cooked with aromatic herbs, spices, and broth, often alongside vegetables and proteins. The grains absorb the flavors of the other ingredients, resulting in a cohesive and flavorful dish. Experimenting with different grains, such as quinoa, farro, or barley, can add variety and nutritional benefits to your meals.

One-pot meals are also well-suited to slow cooking, whether in a slow cooker or a low oven. Slow-cooked dishes like pulled pork or braised short ribs allow tough cuts of meat to become tender and flavorful over several hours of gentle cooking. These dishes are often even better the next day, as the flavors continue to develop and meld. Slow cooking also offers the convenience of hands-off cooking, allowing you to prepare a delicious meal with minimal effort.

In conclusion, one-pot wonders are a testament to the beauty of simplicity and the power of letting ingredients come together in harmony. Whether you're preparing a quick weeknight dinner, a leisurely weekend brunch, or a festive gathering, these dishes offer a practical, flavorful, and often healthier alternative to more complex meals. By mastering the art of layering flavors, balancing textures, and choosing the right pot, you can create a wide range of satisfying and delicious one-pot meals that will delight your family and friends. Embrace the creativity and convenience of one-pot cooking, and discover the endless possibilities that this approach to cooking offers. The joy of one-pot wonders also lies in their adaptability to various dietary preferences and restrictions. Whether you're cooking for vegetarians, vegans, or those with specific food allergies, there are countless ways to tailor these meals to fit everyone's needs without sacrificing flavor or satisfaction.

30-Minute Meals

Life can often feel like a whirlwind, with days packed from dawn till dusk with work, errands, and social commitments. Amid this hustle, finding time to prepare a wholesome, home-cooked meal can seem daunting. Yet, the beauty of 30-minute meals lies in their ability to deliver delicious, nutritious dishes without monopolizing your entire evening. These meals are a testament to the fact that good food doesn't always require hours in the kitchen. With a bit of planning and a few strategic choices, you can whip up a satisfying meal in just half an hour.

The key to mastering 30-minute meals is simplicity and efficiency. This doesn't mean compromising on flavor or nutrition; rather, it involves smart cooking techniques and ingredient choices. Start by focusing on dishes that utilize fresh, high-quality ingredients, which naturally require less manipulation to shine. Think vibrant vegetables, lean proteins, and fragrant herbs and spices that pack a punch.

One effective strategy is to streamline your prep work. Pre-chopping vegetables, pre-marinating meats, and even pre-measuring spices can save precious minutes. Having a well-organized kitchen with easily accessible tools and ingredients also speeds up the cooking process. A sharp knife, a sturdy cutting board, and a few versatile pans can make all the difference.

Stir-fries are a quintessential 30-minute meal. They are quick, versatile, and can be customized to suit any palate. A classic chicken and vegetable stir-fry, for example, can be made by heating a tablespoon of oil in a large pan or wok. Add thinly sliced chicken breast and cook until browned. Remove the chicken and set it aside. In the same pan, add a mix of colorful vegetables like bell peppers, snap peas, and carrots. Stir-fry until they are crisp-tender, then return the chicken to the pan. Add a simple sauce made from soy sauce, garlic, ginger, and a touch of honey or hoisin sauce. Toss everything together until well-coated and heated through. Serve over steamed rice or noodles for a complete meal.

Pasta dishes are another excellent option for quick dinners. They offer endless possibilities and can be as simple or elaborate as you like. A speedy pasta primavera, for instance, celebrates the flavors of fresh vegetables. Start by bringing a pot of salted water to a boil. Cook your choice of pasta according to the package instructions. While the pasta is cooking, heat olive oil in a large pan. Add minced garlic and a medley of chopped vegetables such as zucchini, cherry tomatoes, and asparagus. Sauté until the vegetables are tender. Drain the pasta, reserving a bit of the pasta water. Toss the pasta with the vegetables, adding a splash of the reserved water to create a light sauce. Finish with a generous handful of grated Parmesan cheese and a sprinkle of fresh basil.

Fish is another great protein for 30-minute meals, as it cooks quickly and pairs well with a variety of flavors. A simple pan-seared salmon with lemon-dill sauce can be both elegant and easy. Season salmon fillets with salt and pepper, then sear them in a hot pan with a bit of oil until the skin is crispy and the flesh is opaque. Remove the salmon and set it aside. In the same pan, add a splash of white wine or chicken broth, a squeeze of lemon juice, and a handful of chopped fresh dill. Let it simmer for a few minutes to reduce slightly, then pour the sauce over the salmon. Serve with a side of steamed vegetables or a simple salad.

Salads can also be transformed into satisfying main courses with the right mix of ingredients. A hearty Greek salad with grilled chicken is a perfect example. Start by grilling or pan-searing chicken breasts seasoned with oregano, salt, and pepper. While the chicken is cooking, assemble the salad: combine chopped romaine lettuce, cucumbers, cherry tomatoes, red onion, Kalamata olives, and feta cheese in a large bowl. Whisk together a quick dressing with olive oil, red wine vinegar, garlic, and a bit of Dijon mustard. Slice the cooked chicken and place it on top of the salad, then drizzle with the dressing. This dish is not only quick but also packed with flavor and nutrients.

Soups can be surprisingly quick to prepare, especially if you use pre-made broth or bouillon. A classic tomato basil soup can come together in minutes. Sauté chopped onions and garlic in a bit of olive oil until they are soft and fragrant. Add canned crushed tomatoes and vegetable or chicken broth. Let it simmer for about 20 minutes to allow the flavors to meld. Use an immersion blender to puree the soup until smooth. Stir in a splash of cream and a handful of fresh basil leaves. Serve with a side of crusty bread for a comforting and quick meal.

Tacos are another fantastic option for fast meals. They are fun to assemble and can be customized to suit everyone's tastes. For shrimp tacos, start by tossing peeled and deveined shrimp with a bit of olive oil, chili powder, cumin, and salt. Sauté the shrimp in a hot pan until they are pink and cooked through. Warm some corn tortillas and fill them with the shrimp. Top with a quick slaw made from shredded cabbage, lime juice, and cilantro. Add a dollop of sour cream or a sprinkle of cheese, if desired. These tacos are fresh, flavorful, and ready in no time.

Eggs are often overlooked for dinner, but they can be the star of a quick and satisfying meal. A frittata is a great way to use up leftover vegetables and cheese. Beat a few eggs with a splash of milk, salt, and pepper. Heat an oven-safe pan and sauté any vegetables you have on hand—spinach, mushrooms, and bell peppers work well. Pour the egg mixture over the vegetables and cook until the edges start to set. Sprinkle with cheese and transfer the pan to the oven to finish cooking under the broiler until the top is golden and puffy. Slice and serve with a side salad for a light yet filling dinner.

Finally, sandwiches can be elevated to dinner status with the right ingredients. A Caprese sandwich, for example, can be made by layering fresh mozzarella, ripe tomatoes, and basil leaves on a crusty baguette. Drizzle with balsamic glaze and a bit of olive oil, then season with salt and pepper. Press the sandwich in a panini press or cook in a hot pan until the bread is crispy and the cheese is melted. Serve with a side of mixed greens for a complete meal.

Incorporating these strategies and recipes into your routine can make weeknight dinners both enjoyable and manageable. The key is to embrace simplicity, use high-quality ingredients, and keep your kitchen organized. With a bit of practice, you'll find that preparing a delicious, home-cooked meal in 30 minutes is not only possible but also immensely satisfying. Whether you're cooking for yourself or your family, these quick meals ensure that you can enjoy a nutritious dinner without compromising on time or taste. Batch cooking and meal prepping can be invaluable allies in your quest for efficient 30-minute meals. By dedicating a couple of hours on the weekend to prepare certain components, you can significantly cut down on your weeknight cooking time. For instance, roasting a large batch of vegetables or cooking a pot of quinoa can provide you with versatile ingredients that can be quickly incorporated into various dishes throughout the week. Similarly, marinating meats in advance or even cooking large portions and freezing them can make meal preparation during busy evenings a breeze.

Pasta and Noodle Dishes

Pasta and noodle dishes are beloved worldwide for their versatility, comforting nature, and the sheer joy they bring to our tables. They can be as simple or as elaborate as you wish, making them perfect for both quick weeknight meals and leisurely weekend feasts. Understanding the basic principles and techniques for cooking pasta and noodles can elevate your culinary repertoire, allowing you to create dishes that are both satisfying and impressive.

When it comes to pasta, the Italians have mastered the art, and their influence is seen globally. The foundation of any great pasta dish starts with cooking the pasta correctly. The term "al dente," meaning "to the tooth," describes pasta that is cooked to be firm to the bite. To achieve this, bring a large pot of salted water to a rolling boil before adding the pasta. The salt is crucial as it seasons the pasta from the inside out. Stir the pasta occasionally to prevent sticking and cook it according to the package instructions, checking a minute or two before the suggested time to ensure it doesn't overcook.

One of the simplest yet most delicious pasta dishes is Spaghetti Aglio e Olio. This classic Italian dish requires just a few ingredients: spaghetti, garlic, olive oil, red pepper flakes, and parsley. While the spaghetti cooks, gently sauté thinly sliced garlic in a generous amount of olive oil until it's golden and fragrant. Add a pinch of red pepper flakes for heat. Once the spaghetti is al dente, reserve a cup of the pasta water and drain the rest. Toss the spaghetti in the garlic oil mixture, adding some of the reserved pasta water to create a silky sauce. Finish with chopped parsley and a bit of freshly grated Parmesan cheese if desired. This dish is a perfect example of how simplicity and quality ingredients can create something extraordinary.

For those who enjoy heartier meals, a classic Bolognese sauce is a must-try. This rich, meaty sauce is traditionally served with tagliatelle or pappardelle, but it pairs well with any pasta shape. Start by sautéing finely chopped onions, carrots, and celery in olive oil until they're soft. Add ground beef and cook until browned. Stir in tomato paste and cook for a few minutes to deepen the flavor, then add canned tomatoes, a splash of red wine, and a bit of milk or cream. Let the sauce simmer gently for at least an hour, allowing the flavors to meld. Serve the Bolognese over pasta, garnished with fresh basil and a generous sprinkle of Parmesan.

Shifting to Asian-inspired noodle dishes, there is a vast array of flavors and techniques to explore. One popular dish is Pad Thai, a staple of Thai cuisine. This stir-fried noodle dish combines rice noodles with a sweet and tangy sauce, shrimp or chicken, tofu, eggs, and a variety of vegetables. The key to a great Pad Thai is the sauce, typically made from tamarind paste, fish sauce, sugar, and lime juice. Prepare the sauce in advance to streamline the cooking process. Stir-fry the protein and vegetables, then push them to the side of the pan and scramble the eggs. Add the soaked rice noodles and sauce, tossing everything together until well-coated. Serve with crushed peanuts, fresh bean sprouts, and lime wedges for a vibrant, flavorful meal.

Japanese cuisine offers another treasure trove of noodle dishes, with Ramen being one of the most beloved. While traditional ramen can be a labor-intensive process involving homemade broth and noodles, a simplified version can still deliver satisfying results. Use a good-quality store-bought broth as your base, enhancing it with ingredients like soy sauce, miso, garlic, and ginger. Add cooked ramen noodles, then top with sliced pork, soft-boiled eggs, green onions, and nori. This comforting bowl of noodles is perfect for a quick and nourishing meal.

For those who prefer a lighter option, Vietnamese Pho is an excellent choice. This aromatic noodle soup features a clear broth, typically made from beef or chicken, infused with spices such as star anise, cloves, and cinnamon. While the broth traditionally takes hours to develop its deep flavor, you can achieve a quicker version using pre-made broth and enhancing it with the spices. Serve the hot broth over cooked rice noodles, thinly sliced meat, and fresh herbs like cilantro and basil. Add bean sprouts, lime wedges, and sliced chili for a customizable and refreshing meal.

Exploring Mediterranean flavors, Greek Orzo Salad is a delightful cold pasta dish perfect for warm weather. Orzo, a rice-shaped pasta, is cooked until al dente and then tossed with a medley of fresh vegetables like cucumbers, tomatoes, and red onions. Add Kalamata olives, feta cheese, and a simple dressing made from olive oil, lemon juice, oregano, and garlic. This salad is not only quick to prepare but also incredibly satisfying and packed with vibrant flavors.

Another Mediterranean-inspired dish is Spaghetti with Pesto. Pesto, a fragrant sauce made from fresh basil, garlic, pine nuts, Parmesan cheese, and olive oil, is a fantastic no-cook option for a speedy meal. Simply blend the ingredients in a food processor until smooth. Toss the cooked spaghetti with the pesto, adding a bit of the reserved pasta water to help the sauce coat the noodles evenly. This dish is a celebration of fresh, herbaceous flavors and can be made even more substantial with the addition of grilled chicken or shrimp.

For a twist on traditional pasta, consider incorporating spiralized vegetables as a noodle substitute. Zucchini noodles, or "zoodles," are a popular low-carb alternative that can be used in many pasta dishes. One simple preparation is Zoodles with Marinara Sauce. Spiralize zucchini into noodles and sauté briefly in olive oil until just tender. Top with your favorite marinara sauce and a sprinkle of Parmesan for a light and healthy meal.

Asian-inspired dishes also offer creative ways to use vegetable noodles. For example, Sweet Potato Noodle Stir-Fry combines spiralized sweet potatoes with a savory sauce and a variety of vegetables. Sauté the sweet potato noodles in a hot pan with a bit of oil until tender, then add a mix of bell peppers, snap peas, and mushrooms. Toss everything with a sauce made from soy sauce, sesame oil, garlic, and ginger. This dish is not only colorful and nutritious but also bursting with umami flavors.

Mastering pasta and noodle dishes is all about understanding the balance of flavors and textures. Whether you prefer the rich, comforting sauces of Italian cuisine, the bold and spicy flavors of Asian dishes, or the fresh and vibrant notes of Mediterranean fare, there is a pasta or noodle dish for every taste and occasion. By incorporating these techniques and recipes into your cooking repertoire, you can enjoy a wide variety of delicious meals that are both satisfying and impressive. Experimenting with different pasta shapes and noodle types can also add variety to your meals. Each pasta shape is designed to hold sauces differently, enhancing the overall dining experience. For instance, tubular shapes like penne and rigatoni are perfect for hearty, chunky sauces because they trap the sauce inside. Fusilli, with its spirals, is great for capturing light, creamy sauces or vinaigrettes in pasta salads. Long strands like spaghetti and linguine are ideal for smooth, olive oil-based sauces or simple tomato sauces.

Family-Friendly Casseroles

A warm casserole bubbling away in the oven can be the epitome of comfort food, especially for busy families. Casseroles are not only practical and convenient, but they also offer a delightful way to bring everyone together around the dinner table. Whether you're looking for a weeknight meal that can be assembled quickly or a dish that can be prepared in advance and baked later, family-friendly casseroles are the answer. They are versatile, can be customized to suit various tastes, and often include ingredients that are readily available in your pantry.

One of the great advantages of casseroles is their ability to incorporate a variety of ingredients, making them a nutritious choice for families. They often contain a balance of proteins, vegetables, and carbohydrates, all baked together to create a harmonious dish. This flexibility allows you to sneak in extra vegetables for the kids or use up leftovers in a creative way. For instance, a classic Chicken and Broccoli Casserole combines tender chicken pieces with nutritious broccoli, all enveloped in a creamy sauce and topped with a crunchy breadcrumb crust. This dish not only tastes great but also provides a good mix of protein and fiber.

To get started with making casseroles, it's important to understand some of the basic components that make up these dishes. Typically, a casserole will have a base, which could be pasta, rice, or potatoes. The base provides the bulk of the dish and soaks up the flavors from the other ingredients. Next, a protein source is added—this could be chicken, beef, pork, or even beans for a vegetarian option. Vegetables are then incorporated to add color, texture, and nutrition. Finally, a sauce or binder, such as a creamy cheese sauce, tomato sauce, or even a simple broth, helps to meld the ingredients together and add moisture.

A beloved family-friendly casserole is the Cheesy Beef and Pasta Bake. This dish starts with cooked pasta, such as penne or rotini, mixed with browned ground beef and a medley of vegetables like bell peppers, onions, and spinach. The mixture is then coated in a rich tomato sauce and topped with a generous amount of shredded mozzarella cheese. Baking it in the oven results in a bubbly, cheesy top layer that's irresistible. This casserole is a hit with kids and adults alike and can be easily customized by adding different vegetables or using ground turkey instead of beef.

For a lighter yet equally satisfying option, consider a Vegetable and Quinoa Casserole. Quinoa, a protein-packed grain, serves as the base and is mixed with a variety of roasted vegetables such as zucchini, bell peppers, and cherry tomatoes. A mixture of eggs and milk is poured over to bind everything together, and a sprinkle of feta cheese adds a tangy finish. This casserole is not only nutritious but also gluten-free, making it suitable for those with dietary restrictions. It's a great way to introduce more plant-based meals into your family's diet without compromising on flavor or satisfaction.

Another classic that has stood the test of time is Tuna Noodle Casserole. This dish is simple to prepare and can be made with pantry staples, making it a go-to for busy weeknights. Cooked egg noodles are combined with canned tuna, peas, and a creamy mushroom sauce, then topped with buttery breadcrumbs. Baking it until golden brown creates a comforting, creamy dish that's sure to please even the pickiest eaters. For an added twist, try using whole wheat noodles and adding some shredded carrots or chopped spinach for extra nutrition.

Casseroles are also an excellent way to incorporate leftovers into a new meal. For example, a Turkey and Stuffing Casserole can be a wonderful way to use up holiday leftovers. Shredded turkey is mixed with leftover stuffing, green beans, and a creamy gravy, then baked until hot and bubbly. This dish not only minimizes food waste but also brings back the flavors of a festive meal in a convenient one-dish format.

For a more indulgent option, consider making a Loaded Baked Potato Casserole. This dish captures all the flavors of a loaded baked potato but in casserole form, making it easier to serve a crowd. Start with a base of mashed potatoes, then layer on cooked bacon, shredded cheddar cheese, chopped green onions, and a dollop of sour cream. Bake until the cheese is melted and bubbly. This casserole is sure to be a hit at family gatherings or potlucks.

When it comes to preparing casseroles, planning and organization can make the process smoother. Many casseroles can be assembled ahead of time and stored in the refrigerator or freezer until you're ready to bake them. This makes them an excellent option for meal prep. For instance, you can assemble a Chicken Enchilada Casserole the night before and simply pop it in the oven when you get home from work. Layers of corn tortillas, shredded chicken, black beans, corn, and enchilada sauce are topped with cheese and baked until hot and bubbly. Serve with a side of Spanish rice and a green salad for a complete meal.

To ensure your casseroles turn out perfectly every time, consider a few key tips. First, when using vegetables with high water content, such as zucchini or mushrooms, try to sauté them first to remove some of the moisture. This will prevent your casserole from becoming too watery. Second, if you're adding a crunchy topping, such as breadcrumbs or crushed crackers, drizzle them with a bit of melted butter before baking to ensure they turn golden brown. Finally, let your casserole rest for a few minutes after baking before serving. This allows the ingredients to set and makes it easier to slice and serve.

Casseroles are not only practical but also a great way to bring creativity into the kitchen. You can experiment with different flavor combinations and ingredients to suit your family's preferences. For example, a Greek-inspired casserole could include layers of orzo pasta, ground lamb, spinach, and a creamy béchamel sauce, topped with crumbled feta cheese. Or try a Tex-Mex Chicken and Rice Casserole with layers of spicy chicken, black beans, corn, and rice, topped with cheddar cheese and fresh cilantro.

Involving children in the preparation of casseroles can also be a fun and educational activity. Kids can help with tasks such as layering ingredients, sprinkling cheese, or mixing sauces. This not only makes cooking a family affair but also helps children learn valuable kitchen skills and develop a love for homemade meals.

In conclusion, family-friendly casseroles are a versatile and convenient option for busy households. They can be tailored to various tastes and dietary needs, making them a go-to for any occasion. Whether you're looking for a quick weeknight dinner or a dish to bring to a potluck, casseroles offer endless possibilities. By incorporating a balance of proteins, vegetables, and carbohydrates, you can create nutritious and satisfying meals that your family will love. So, embrace the art of casserole making and enjoy the comfort and joy these dishes bring to your table. Another delightful casserole that is sure to become a family favorite is the Baked Ziti. This Italian-American classic is hearty and comforting, perfect for a Sunday family dinner or a potluck gathering. Start by cooking ziti pasta until al dente, then mix it with a generous amount of marinara sauce and ricotta cheese. Layer the pasta mixture with mozzarella cheese and a sprinkle of Parmesan, then bake until the cheese is melted and bubbly. To add more depth of flavor, consider incorporating Italian sausage or ground beef into the sauce. The result is a

rich, cheesy, and deeply satisfying dish that pairs
wonderfully with a simple green salad and garlic
bread.